YOU'RE FAMOUS, WHY ME?

"UNTIL THE BLACK MAN IS ALLOWED TO REJECT THIS DEMAND FOR STRENGTH, HE WILL NEVER TRULY EXPERIENCE HIS OWN HUMANITY."

Herbert "Shawn" Miller

Copyright © 2024 Herbert "Shawn" Miller
All rights reserved

Introduction

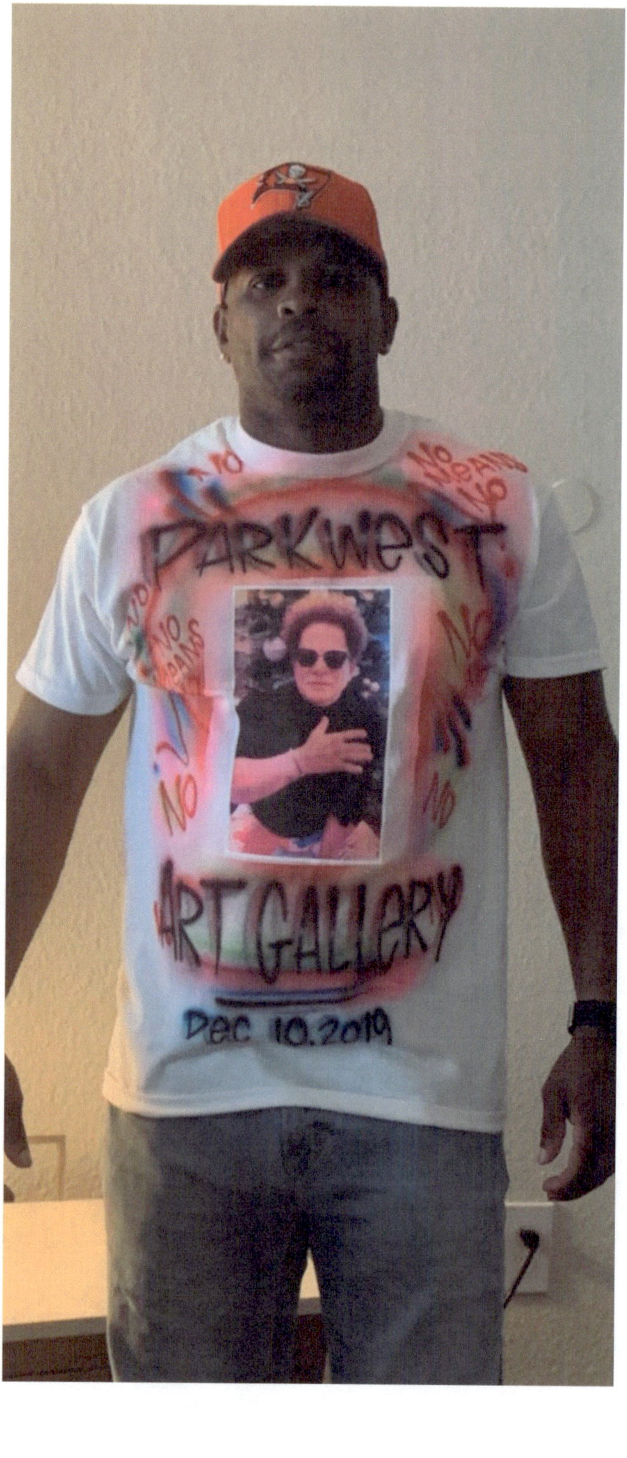
PARKWEST
ART GALLERY
Dec 10.2019

The Boat

"I did what my conscience told me to do, and you can't fail if you do that."

- Anita Hill

ON DECEMBER 10, 2019, two days after I followed the gangway aboard the Norwegian Encore, my life changed forever. As VIP art collectors, my wife and I were invited on a complimentary cruise to participate in a Park West Art Gallery event. Our invitation came as no surprise, as we have been avid art collectors for over a decade. Each wall in our home is dedicated to a well-known artist, and the high walls are covered in framed paintings from top to bottom. The wall just inside and across from the front entrance of our house is adorned with pieces from the acclaimed Brazilian pop artist Romero Britto. His child-like use of shapes and bright colors caught our attention. His work was full of life and conveyed messages of love, joy, and happiness. My wife and I were happy to know that such lively paintings would be some of the first works of art we'd ever collect. We were even more pleased to learn that Romero Britto would be aboard the Norwegian Encore. Park West's promise of access to some of the most exclusive artworks in their gallery aboard their VIP cruise and the opportunity to meet various artists, to understand who they are as people, and to learn more about their approaches to painting excited us the same way meeting a movie star would thrill a film buff. We were eager to meet and speak to the people who talked to us through their images. And we were fortunate for the opportunity to do it at the personal level Park West was offering.

Had I known just forty-eight hours earlier that pulling my suitcase up the metal ramp to head out to sea would mean reframing who I was as a man, brick by brick, I would have turned in the opposite direction. I have never been one to run, but I would have grabbed my wife by the hand and run the other way. Looking back,

HERBERT "SHAWN" MILLER

I wish I had. Never boarding the ship at all would have been better than walking into our home and being greeted by a now naked wall, would have been better than being forced to question my worth as a human being, and knowing with vivid clarity just how hard it is to move when everything in you is screaming, "Run!"

"Strong Black Man"

While the Strong Black Man insignia charades as a compliment it really pardons the rest of the world of their responsibility to view the Black Man as vulnerable, able to experience pain, capable of weakness, worthy of support, and unconditional love. Until the Bl Black Man is allowed to reject this demand for strength, he will never truly experience his own humanity.

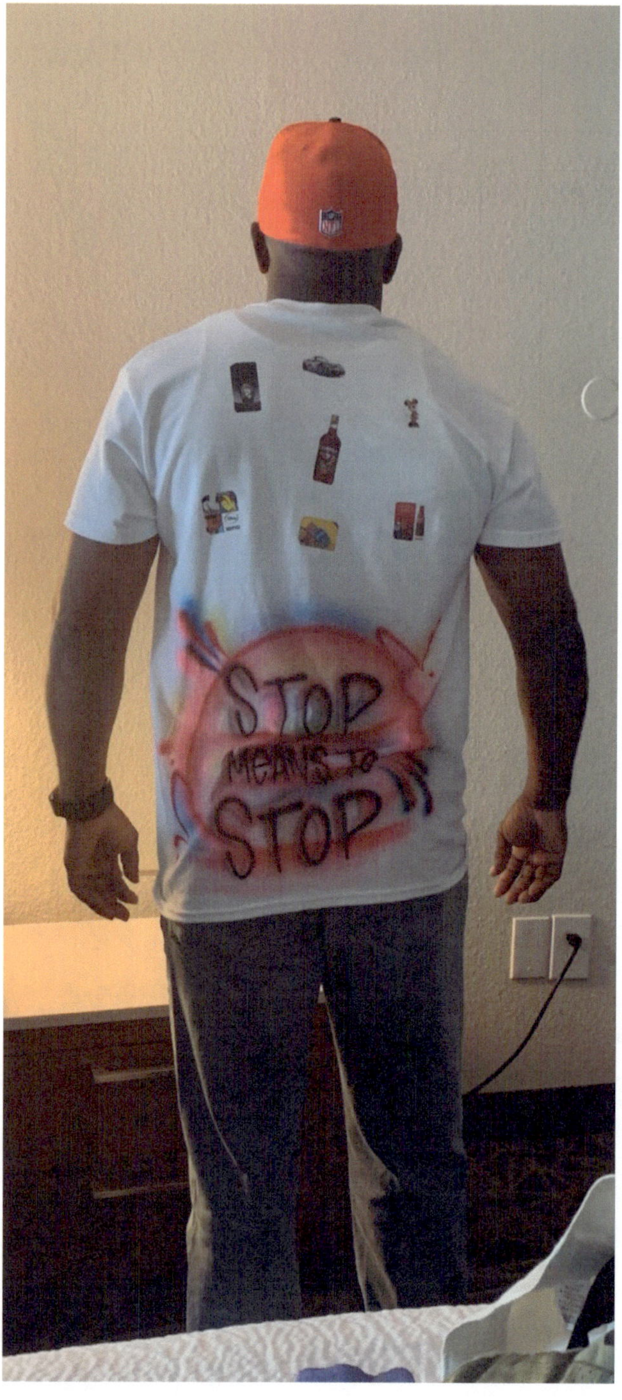
STOP
MEANS TO
STOP

Chapter 1

IN 2019, CNN announced that Romero Britto was the most-licensed artist. He has been recognized and embraced by the Pope, Michael Jackson, the Bush Family, Sugar Ray Leonard, Whitney Houston, and Barack Obama. Romero Britto has enjoyed the bounty of high-end endorsements from Absolut Vodka, Walt Disney, Coca-Cola, Mattel Luggage, Chiquita Banana, and Maserati. The come-from-nothing artist used his creative passion to inspire the hearts of millions with whimsical imagery, vibrant colors, and bold patterns. But I know the world-renowned pop painter as a predator.

You can never judge a book by its cover. Similarly, you can never judge a painting by its artist. To tie an artist to his work is a dangerous thing to do; I could have never known that the man that envisions such upbeat artworks could be the same man I'd hauntingly and unwillingly get to know on a life-shattering December morning. Even today, I'd be wary of saying I know Romero Britto. Still, I know this: Romero Britto is a sexual predator, manipulator, coercer, and the person who held me hostage in his cabin room for over an hour.

One of the most alluring parts of this trip was the opportunity to meet three famous artists. The itinerary was set in place on the first night, and on December 8, 2019, Romero Britto joined the gallery VIPs in the Auction Room and spoke to a small group of art enthusiasts, which included my wife and I. His Senior Account Executive, Katherine Davis, used her phone to record his entrance, and Britto took the time to greet each of the art auctioneers before turning his attention to the crowd. At that point, I saw Britto in an admirable light. He shared with us his life story: he lived in a small city in Brazil and had a large family—he was one of twelve children. He told us he'd led a difficult life, but he was thankful he had achieved success. He'd persevered through tough times, but he assured the group he had never forgotten where he came from. He inspired everyone, me included, when he ended this portion of his remarks by saying he'd achieved his goals by doing what made him feel happy and what he brought to others.

The night carried on later than expected, but nobody seemed to mind. After he addressed the smaller gathering and took a break,

WHY ME?

Britto then returned to greet a larger group in one of the other event rooms.

He spoke and behaved in a down-to-earth way that almost allowed me to relate on a personal level with the multi-million-dollar artist. He stepped on stage in a colorful, playing card-covered suit that spoke to the artist's loud style and outspoken personality. With the mic in one hand, he laughingly told us how tired he was.

"Got on the ship and went straight to my cabin and went to sleep." He continued, "I haven't gotten to take a shower in a few days. I traveled from Europe to get on this ship, but I'm happy to be here with you guys."

The crowd laughed in an awkward way, how people sometimes do when they're a little shocked and not sure whether laughter is an appropriate response, but everyone seemed to respect the artist and appreciate his honesty. After sharing a few more stories with the crowd, Britto turned to Jordan, one of the ship's senior auctioneers. For the next several minutes, Britto talked about his accomplishments and upcoming endeavors.

At this point, the night started to die down. I left, feeling as if Romero Britto was an all-around good guy. I looked forward to meeting him at the next event.

By the time December 9th rolled around, my wife and I had become acquainted with a few other passengers. We had lunch with another art-collecting couple we met the night prior. I made plans to join a poker tournament with a group of gallery VIPs. By now, we'd had time to explore and become familiar with the ship, and we looked forward to an eventful Monday. There was much to do aboard the brand-new Encore, but we were most awaiting Park West's Meet the Artist event. This wasn't our first time being a part of such a distinguished art gala. Still, it was our first opportunity to meet Romero Britto, and after witnessing his demeanor the other night—not to mention having collected his artwork for over a decade—we could hardly contain our excitement. During events like these in the past, we've met Peter Max, Scott Jacobs and Marcus Glenn. Our dedication to collecting had led us to one of my most memorable moments—the day we traveled to Palm Harbor, Florida, to meet our most beloved artist Peter Max. The story behind that trip is kind of interesting.

My wife and daughters and I had taken a trip abroad on a Norwegian cruise ship—a vacation I'll remember fondly for the rest of my life. We traveled several times a year out of the country, collecting art and wine. Through trial and error, we discovered NCL was the only way to go. They provided impeccable customer service, and the employees on the boat always made my girls feel right at home.

On this cruise we introduced our daughters to the world of art collection in the realest, most tangible way. For the first time, we allowed each of the girls to bid on art that sparked their interest—with some guidance of course. My twenty-year-old daughter was hooked instantly. She bought two paintings and enjoyed the free wine. My nine-year-old daughter was no stranger to the world of auctions; she was the only one of our kids who'd joined us when we'd made most of our purchases. She caught on to the bidding process quickly. They each had their own bid card, and I would give them a look that meant it was okay to bid on a certain piece if they wanted to, or I would shake my head when a piece came up that I didn't think was worth buying or if a bid went beyond what I felt a piece was worth. They both loved every minute of the auctions…the thrill of the fast-paced bidding and the feeling of prestige and satisfaction that came with being an art collector. But enough about the girls and their love for their art. Clearly, we are an art-loving family.

This trip was memorable not only because the girls purchased their first artwork, but also, we spent much more money than I had intended. I'd thought I would get away with forking out maybe twenty-five thousand dollars or so, but my wife and daughters had other plans. On our last night onboard, we were invited to see a one-of-one Peter Max creation. I was not with the family that evening, and they went to view the unique piece without me. By the time I did see them, it was already too late. My wife fell in love with the work the moment she saw it, and my family decided we needed it in our collection. The next day, during the final auction, the acrylic painting by Peter Max was unveiled, and the auctioneer told the story behind the work of art, which the artist had named *Susan*.

WHY ME?

According to the story, Peter Max was experiencing the first symptoms of Alzheimer's. He was married to a much younger wife, and he and this woman had an understanding. They lived next door to each other, and Peter allowed his wife to have a boyfriend closer to her age. When his wife realized Peter was becoming forgetful, she and her boyfriend convinced Peter to sign many of his paintings, and then she sold them online and kept all the profits. During this time, Peter had a live-in caregiver. When the caregiver realized Peter was being taken advantage of, she took him to live in an undisclosed location in the hopes of protecting him from his wife's predatory behavior. Peter's wife was livid when she came home to find him gone. For nearly a year, the caregiver kept Peter hidden in a remote location. His wife filed a kidnapping charge against the caregiver, only to learn that the woman was a law student or an attorney and had gone through all the proper legal steps to ensure Peter's safety and well-being, as well as her own. The kidnapping charges were thrown out, and Peter was returned to his family; soon after, they fired the caregiver. During his seclusion, Peter had created only one painting: *Susan*. Park West told us Susan was the name of a woman Peter had been madly in love with—the one that had gotten away. Of course, this was many, many years earlier in his life. When my family heard this part of the painting's provenance, it cemented their decision to purchase *Susan* and add it to our collection.

Coincidentally, shortly after deciding to purchase the painting, we got the opportunity to meet Peter Max face-to-face. Peter was visiting a studio in Palm Harbor, and we planned to meet him and ask him to sign the painting. I will never forget that encounter, because Peter Max changed my life and how I felt about art. He was talking with a group of art collectors when my wife, her parents, and I walked through the door. Peter stopped mid-sentence and started pointing and waving in my direction. I turned to see who he was gesturing at, but there was no one else behind or around me, other than my wife. For some reason, he wanted me to join him. As I approached him, nervous, my hands sweating, and unable to think of what to say, the whole room gawked at me. He reached up with both hands, grabbed my face, and kissed my cheeks.

"Now you are my new best friend," he whispered.

I had no words to express my thoughts. I was the only Black person at the event, and he had singled me out. He signed everything I had brought with me and spent more time with me than the sponsors of the art gallery. He wouldn't leave my side or let me go. It was a life-changing experience. In my family's eyes, Peter Max is truly a hero.

Back onboard the Norwegian Encore, I thought back to that meeting. If the great Peter Max could declare to a room full of people that I was his "new best friend," then getting to know Romero Britto a little better seemed like a possibility.

The Meet and Greet began, and the room buzzed with excited anticipation. It was midday when the artist walked into the room for the VIP 101 event as one of the featured artists. My wife Kelly and I approached the artist when our turn came and exchanged ordinary pleasantries. Kelly told him how much we enjoyed his art, and we both talked about how his artwork had captured our imaginations and how purchasing one of his paintings had kick-started our venture into the world of art collection. In our brief but pleasant encounter, we also mentioned our three daughters back home and how much they would have loved to be on this boat with us. We captured the moment with a few pictures then left the meet and greet, saying we hoped to see each other around the ship.

The night carried on like any other night on a cruise. Kelly and I partook in a few of the amenities, went to dinner, and as it got a little later, we parted ways. Kelly is an early to bed type and also somewhat of an introvert; in this way, we've always been opposites. I have always been a night owl and a social butterfly. My friends and family refer to me as the "life of the party," so when my wife decided to head back to our cabin around 10:00 p.m., she wasn't upset or suprised that I didn't join her. Instead, I went back to the Poker Table, played a few hours, and then left the casino. I explored the massive boat and eventually found my way to a social club illuminated by strobe lights and blaring Latin music. Earlier in the evening, I had agreed to meet three VIP members Kelly and I had become fairly friendly with at the auctions. I came in and sat at a table. I took my jacket off and hung it on the back of the chair and set my bottled water down on the table, then I stood up and looked around the party lounge. The dance floor was small and adjacent to the bar. The energy drew me in as I weaved my way through the maze of plush lounge chairs. I saw a few familiar faces at the bar and a few more on the dance floor, including the famous Romero Britto. I walked up to the ladies I'd agreed to meet. They were on the dance floor, but they weren't dancing. Instead, they were looking at Britto, their mouths hanging open. Britto was dancing provocatively with another man—no big deal, except this guy clearly looked underage.

Even from afar, I could tell that everyone in the group was visibly drunk.

Wow, they know how to party, I thought.

I've never been much of a drinker—I've never really liked the taste or the feeling of not having full control of my mental and physical faculties. But I approached the group anyway, because we all had something in common—art. As I got closer, I realized everyone at the bar was watching Britto on the dancefloor. The other patrons laughed and drank and ordered more rounds, all while keeping an eye on the Miami-based painter dancing with a young man in the middle of the room. I turned my attention to the dancefloor, too, and shook my head. Why wasn't Britto's PR team or Park West Gallery's auctioneers doing something to intervene? Why would they allow the super-successful artist to create a potential scandal? Here was this middle-aged Brazilian man, belligerently drunk, dancing provocatively with another, much-younger Spanish guy. If a tabloid got ahold of this information, they could ruin the man's reputation. And things only got worse from there. Britto kept putting his hands on his dance partner and even tried to take off the guy's clothes.

The whole situation turned my stomach, and I shook my head and watched in disbelief. The ladies I'd arranged to meet there seemed equally shocked.

As the night carried on Jordan, Katherine, and the rest of Britto's group cheered him on from the sidelines and ran up his tab, ordering drink after drink. They toasted the artist of the hour and laughed as they watched Britto behaving like a pervert in public. The two men danced together for hours, breaking apart only to make more trips to the bar or visit the young man's group of friends with more rounds of drinks. Britto took turns occupying space in each area and rotating from the bar to the table where the young group sat. I roamed around the room, circling from my table back to the bar where the other VIPs sat, and I even spent some time on the dancefloor. Britto bought drinks for everyone in the room. The perfect host, he kept the liquor coming. He offered me several glasses throughout the night, and I politely explained that I don't drink, but as Britto's intoxication became more robust, my refusals meant less to him. Each time he brought me a drink, I left it on my table or gave it to another person standing at the bar. I figured there was no need to let a free drink go to waste. I found my way back to the table with the other ladies and considered turning in. Just as I began to think my night was coming to an end, Britto came over to our table and asked me to help him take Katherine, a woman who worked for him as a senior account executive, back to her room.

I glanced over at the woman in question and sighed. She appeared way too intoxicated to go wandering around the ship alone, and I guessed I had no choice but to assist. Not only had Britto asked me specifically, but I didn't want to be responsible for a drunk woman tumbling overboard.

As we half-carried Katherine out into the hallway, one of us on either side of her, holding her up by her upper arms, I wondered what I'd just gotten myself into.

My chivalrous gesture turned into a drawn-out, frustrating venture. Katherine and I barely knew each other, but rather than allow a severely intoxicated woman and an equally intoxicated man become distressed, I had agreed to walk with the two of them to her room. However, I hadn't thought about the fact that I had no idea where her cabin was, and shortly after we left the bar, I learned they had no idea where her cabin was, either.

Britto dug a tiny, folded square of paper out of his jacket pocket and handed it to me.

"Here," he said, "you're in charge of reading the map."

WHY ME?

I unfolded the paper and stared at a smudged, wrinkled mess of notes and arrows, which I could barely decipher. We weren't going to get much help there, and the senior account executive was so far gone, she could hardly put together a sentence to direct us to her door.

We walked aimlessly as she gave us jumbled cabin numbers and guided us to the wrong floors. She giggled up and down the elevator and draped her arm around my shoulder as her legs began to give way from under her. Britto and I struggled to keep her upright as we continued to search for her room. We looked for the room she gave us, 1052, only to find out shortly afterward that the room didn't exist. After endless appearances at cookie-cutter doors, we finally caught the attention of two security guards, and they were able to locate Katherine's room via her door keycard. The security guards helped us find the right room and stuck around long enough to watch Katherine's boss and I put Katherine into her bed. We laid her keycard on the nightstand. Surprisingly enough, Katherine's room was only a few doors down from my own.

I felt good about knowing we had delivered Katherine safely to her cabin, but damn, that was too much like work! Feeling like I'd run a marathon, I was ready to do what all the rest of the Park West team had done and turn in for the night. I'd been feeling okay when Britto asked me to help out, but now it was getting late, and I was starting to feel tired.

Unfortunately, I couldn't go directly to my room because I'd left my belongings back at the bar. I got into the elevator with Britto, pushed the button for the sixth floor, and waited for the metal doors to close. In a horror movie, the main character is always blissfully oblivious. They have no idea everything is about to go horribly wrong. When I look back, I can pinpoint this exact moment as the pivotal event, the instant when everything started to change. If this were a movie, a theater full of people would have screamed, "Get out of there, you stupid idiot!"

But I wasn't an actor, and I watched the doors closed and smiled as the car made its way up.

HERBERT "SHAWN" MILLER

Chapter 2

WE RETURNED TO the lounge, and the same Latin music blared through the speakers, but as we turned the corner, I realized the place had all but emptied. Everyone from Park West had cleared out, leaving behind only a few stragglers.

A quick glance at the time, and I understand why. Helping Katherine took much longer than I'd expected, and it's time for last call. Britto and I part ways, and I head toward my old table to grab my jacket and water bottle.

Suddenly, my attention is drawn to a small commotion at the bar. At the center of the chaos was world-renowned artist Romero Britto…my new liquor-guzzling, alcohol-sharing "friend." I head over to see what's happening.

The young Spanish man—the one Britto pawed on the dancefloor half the night—and his friends were getting ready to leave the club. Britto asked if he could buy them all one more drink. After spending the night dancing with him, the young man accepted, so Britto walked up to the bartender and then gestured to the young man and asked him what he wanted. The Spanish man stays with his friends but yells his order, loud enough for Britto to hear over the music.

The bartender called over to the table of young people, addressing the Spanish-man. "Can I see your I.D.?"

After spending the night running up an alcohol tab large enough to supply a frat party, the young guy responded, "I didn't ask for a drink."

He turned to his friends and laughed, but the bartender must have assumed this interaction meant the man was underage. The bartender summoned the security guard and pointed to their table. As the guard walked in their direction, the group of young people jumped up and scurried out of the club.

Everything happened quickly, and by the time I made it to where Britto stood at the edge of the bar, he had two drinks in his hand and no one to give the second one to.

"Hey, Romero," I said, intending to say goodbye.

He turned to me with a big smile. "Hey, Shawn! Have a drink with me!" He spoke like we were old friends, and he was eager to catch up on what I'd been doing all these years.

"No, thanks." I shook my head, politely declining yet another drink.

Britto shrugged then turned to three men sitting on stools beside him. "How about one of you? Anyone need a drink?"

All three of the guys shook their heads.

"No, thanks. We're good," the closest man said.

"Well, at least let me pay the tab for whatever you're drinking now," Britto said.

The three men offered friendly smiles, but the guy who'd spoken up a moment ago shook his head.

"That's really nice of you," he said, "but we bought the all-inclusive deal when we booked our trip, so all our drinks are already covered."

The three guys finished their drinks and got up to leave. I waited for Britto to turn his attention back to me so I could say something about Katherine and tell him goodnight. He chugged both the drinks he'd bought and then turned his stool to face me.

"Hey, Shawn!" he exclaimed again, almost as if he'd forgotten he'd greeted me just a couple minutes ago.

"Hey, Buddy, I just came over to say goodbye."

"Thanks for helping me with Katherine," he said. "That turned into quite an adventure. I think we saw every cabin door on this ship!"

We both laughed, and I shook my head.

"She might need to slow down on the alcohol some. Next time, there might not be anyone nice around to make sure she gets back to her room safely. Besides," I added, not wanting to end the conversation on a downer, "That was one heck of a difficult job! I thought we'd still be wandering around looking for her cabin at sunrise!"

We laughed together once more, and he babbled a bit about something or other—I really don't recall the exact conversation—but I sat with him and listened as the bartender announced final call.

At that point, Britto turned and handed me a pair of eyeglasses...the same ones he'd been wearing all evening.

"I want you to have these, Shawn; you're my buddy." He nodded as if to underscore the statement. "Why don't you put them on, and we'll take a few photos together?"

I was moved by the kind, though rather odd gesture, and I nodded. "Thanks."

"And to thank you for your help with Katherine, I'd like to create a portrait of you and your family for free.", Britto offered.

Speechless, I stared at him in amazement.

"Give me your phone, and I'll add my number to your contacts." He held out his hand.

Giddy with excitement on the inside—I couldn't wait to get back to our cabin and tell my wife that my new good friend, Romero Britto, wanted to paint a custom portrait of our family—I somehow managed to keep it together enough to murmur a thanks and hand over my cellphone.

As he put his number into my phone, he said, "I remember you said you have a young daughter… I was thinking about getting her one of these." He held up his wrist to display a bracelet he was wearing with the word *HAPPY*. "Do you think she'd like it?"

Once again, I had a hard time forming a coherent thought. Somehow, despite being pretty inebriated at that point, Britto had recalled a tiny detail I'd shared with him hours earlier during the meet and greet. Not only that, but he wanted to buy my youngest child a gift.

He handed my phone back. "Call me tomorrow to set up an appointment about the painting." He'd started slurring his speech a little, and he stumbled and had to grab onto the bar as he finished speaking.

Thinking the man was in just as bad a condition as Katherine had been earlier, I made a spontaneous decision.

"I'll walk you back to your room, okay?" I said. Even though I was dead tired by then, Britto had been extremely kind and generous. Helping him get back to his cabin seemed like the least I could do.

We exited the lounge and walked from there toward the opposite end of the ship. Britto slung one arm over my shoulder, and I supported half of his weight as he stumbled along the corridor. Mid-ship we passed the multi-floor-high Christmas tree, and Britto paused.

"Wanna take a picture with me in front of the tree?"

I didn't need to be asked twice. I pulled out my phone but then thought a moment and said, "Can we take a video instead?" Hoping I wasn't pushing my luck, I added, "And maybe you could tell my daughters, Alaya and Jayla, hello and wish my oldest—that's Alaya—happy birthday?"

Britto didn't even blink. "Sure," he said and sat near the tree.

I joined him and made sure we could both be seen in the frame and then I pressed the record button on the phone.

"Happy Birthday, Alaya. All the amazing things for you and your entire family. Hello, Jayla."

I stopped the recording and stuck the phone back in my pocket, grinning like a fool. Wait until Kelly saw that!

We continued our trek down the length of the ship. Walking Britto to his room proved to be just as time-consuming and laborious as getting Katherine to hers. My body ached, and I was eager to get back to my room and share with my wife the details of my eventful night, our exciting commission, and the personalized video on my phone.

I half-carried the Brazilian man to the elevator, and we headed up to the highest level of the ship. By the time we reached his floor and stepped off the elevator, the alcohol in his blood had begun to take over, and I began to carry more of his weight than he did. Still, he acted upbeat and friendly. The entire way to his room he raved about his incredible view. He talked about it all the way down the hall, stretching his arms in an effort to show the amount of shoreline he could take in from his balcony and speaking in child-like awe over the beautiful scenery. I continued to walk him toward his door, and as we got closer he insisted repeatedly that I needed to come in and stand on his balcony and take in his view. I must admit my interest was piqued. And that was what led me to follow Romero Britto into his suite that night.

I am retelling my story from the perspective of a man who's had more than a few years to analyze this moment, and I am still haunted by the fact I had no idea the night was no longer going in my favor. As the door to Britto's cabin closed behind me, the evening changed.

HERBERT "SHAWN" MILLER

Chapter 3

WHAT HAUNTS ME most of all, to this day, is "Why Me?" What will stay with me and never shake from my core is the smell. It hit me in the nose the moment I entered behind Britto, and I nearly turned and walked out. My stomach lurched. What the heck was that? Worse than any gym locker room I'd ever been in.

The door clicked as the cabin's lock engaged, and Britto spoke to me from the bathroom adjacent to the entry area.

"Go out on the balcony, Shawn. It's amazing. Go see for yourself."

I walked across the room toward the other door, and Britto came out of the bathroom behind me. He kicked off his shoes, flinging them into the middle of the floor. I opened the sliding glass door and stepped out onto a tiny balcony that hung over the front of the ship. I had to suck in several deep breaths to clear my senses of the stench before I could focus on the view, but when I did, I stood in awe. Britto was right; the view from here was amazing, made more intense by the knowledge I hung suspended high above the ocean. I stretched my arms out and pretended I was a part of that iconic scene in the Titanic. I had never experienced anything as fantastic and awe-inspiring as this. Like standing on the edge of the world. Even in the darkness, I could feel miles and miles of ocean surrounding me.

I took in the view and drew a deep breath. Hands came around me from behind, and I gasped and looked over my shoulder.

Romero Britto had come up behind me. Shirtless, wearing only a pair of jeans, he pressed against me from behind and started pulling on the fabric of my shirt, trying to tug it loose from the waistband of my jeans.

"No! Cut it out, man. I'm not like that!" I tried to move away from him, but there really wasn't anywhere to go. The balcony was small, and Britto stood between me and the entrance to the cabin.

As if I hadn't even spoken, Britto continued to try to take off my shirt, and I kept resisting.

"Stop!" I took a side-step and managed to get out of his reach for a moment.

But Britto adjusted his attack and came at me from the front, grabbing and pulling at my shirt. Anger mixed with panic inside me, building at an alarming rate, and I grabbed his wrists and held them as I took a mental step back.

If I let my emotions get the best of me and tried to overpower the man, I might knock him over the railing. I had no way to explain why or how I'd come to be in his room, and if something happened to such a famous person, no one would listen to what I had to say.

Britto managed to free himself from my grip and went right back to tugging on my shirt. A man on a mission, it seemed he'd not be deterred. I looked around for a way out of this mess and realized that in his attempt to get my clothes off, Britto had moved and was leaning against the rail. Not good…

Once again, I stepped around him, putting myself between my attacker and the endless ocean below. Britto had drank all night. One drunken stumble, and he could tumble over the rail and disappear into the darkness below. I was stone-cold sober. Even if he fell into me, I could hang onto the railing to keep from going over.

Britto acted as if he'd lost track of where we were and had only one thing on his mind. He hadn't said a word since he'd come up behind me, but he hadn't stopped reaching for and pulling on my shirt, either. Things went on like this for what seemed like an hour, with him trying to disrobe me, and me resisting, telling him to stop, and struggling to keep my cool so neither of us ended up overboard.

How the heck had I gotten myself into this situation? Blocked from all sides, I fought for calm as the panicky sensation started to grow. I needed to get off that balcony before something really bad happened.

In my shocked and emotionally damaged state, I did the only thing I thought might work. I stopped fighting Britto's attempts at getting my shirt off and stood like a statue, allowing him to drag it up and over my head.

While he seemed distracted by my newly cooperative behavior, I allowed him to lead me back into the cabin. As we stepped inside, he tossed my shirt into a corner of the balcony, and I chose that moment to break free. I hurried straight into little bathroom and closed and locked the door behind me.

I leaned my bare back against the cold door and took a few deep breaths. Now what? I couldn't stay in there for the rest of the cruise, and I didn't want to leave without my shirt. I had no idea what Britto was capable of, what story he might concoct, or if he might seek some kind of revenge against me for scorning his advances. A part of me kept screaming to get the hell out of that cabin, but another part wanted me to try to appease him, to end the situation amicably. I didn't want him to be angry. Maybe this was all just a drunken mistake in judgment on his part? At this time, I raised my hands in the air as I asked God to help me. While talking to God and myself it was loud enough that Britto yelled through the bathroom door asking me, "What did you say?", and "Are you okay?" I quickly replied, "Yes, I'm okay and I'll be right out". When I brought my arms down, from my plea to God for guidance, my left hand hit my left jeans front pocket. At that very moment, I realized my phone was in that pocket. I took it out deciding to video record whatever came next until I was able to exit this cabin. I decided to leave the bathroom and see if I could talk sense to the man.

When I entered the main part of the cabin, Britto was lying across the bed in his white briefs.

"Will you give me a massage?" he mumbled; his face pressed into a pillow.

At that point, I placed my phone face down on the nightstand. With that, I was willing to do whatever it took to get out of that room as quickly as possible and without making Britto angry enough to hold a grudge. Most drunk people fell asleep quickly once they were lying down, especially during a relaxing massage. I decided I'd push on his back for a few minutes and then leave. I stood at the edge of the bed frame, and the mattress pressed against my knees. I had to lean pretty far to reach him, but no way was I getting onto that bed with him. I started pushing on his back, praying he'd pass out soon, but Britto reached for the switch on the LED lights at the head of his bed. He dimmed them, and as he settled back onto the bed, I leaned up and turned them back to full brightness. A moment later, Britto dimmed the lights again, and I sighed before turning them back up.

WHY ME?

This went on for several minutes, and I began to wonder if he had something planned. Why did he need the cover of darkness?

Britto mumbled something into his pillow. He hung horizontally across the bed with his feet dangling off the end.

"What?" I asked, leaning down closer so I could hear him. I didn't want to disturb him and draw him out of his stupor.

As I inched closer, Britto grabbed my hand pulling me onto the bed as he turned over to face me asking, "Can you suck my dick, Shawn?"

Immediately, I recoiled. "No, no, no!" My brain didn't seem capable of forming any other response. Even though he'd tried to remove my shirt and maybe I shouldn't have been surprised, his question shocked me to my core. Terror settled in my chest, and my heart raced. With that one sentence, he turned me into an emotional hostage.

"No," I repeated, louder this time. "No, no, no, no, no!"

Hysteria built up inside me, and my throat closed. Why me? What had I done to draw this kind of attention? Had I given off the wrong kind of signals?

Britto had put me into a position that made me feel stuck. Although he hadn't tied me up or physically forced me to stay—at least, not yet—he held me captive, nonetheless.

A part of my mind signaled I had a choice, that I could leave. *You're a grown man, and you could probably take this guy in a fight if you had to. Just walk out. Go grab your shirt and leave...* But a stronger voice, a frightened voice inside me said I better not dare. *Don't make him mad. You'll be in so much trouble if you make him angry. Just play along. Appease him. He'll pass out eventually and you can leave.*

The fear and anger warred inside me. Up until that moment, I had tried to excuse his behavior. He drank too much. Tomorrow, he probably wouldn't remember any of this. I told myself everything I possibly could to convince myself that I wasn't a victim and that a man I'd idolized for years wasn't going to use his power, fame, and money to try to sexually assault me.

"I-I I need to use the bathroom." I spun around and hurried into the other room, closed and locked the door behind me.

Think, think, think! What the hell is wrong with you? Why are you staying and allowing this man to subject you to this horror?

The answer came instantly but made little sense. I was afraid. Too afraid to save myself from further abuse and humiliation. At that moment, I couldn't have forced myself to walk out the door, and that thought scared me even more.

The thought occurred to me that I may not be able to escape just yet, but the phone on the nightstand could be used for my protection should the events take a turn for the worst.

I took a couple of deep breaths and then opened the bathroom door. I planned to make a dash for the balcony and retrieve my shirt—when I did leave, I didn't want to leave any evidence behind, plus, I needed to cover myself—but when I stepped out and rounded the corner into the cabin, I froze. Britto lay across the bed, completely nude now, and he was masturbating. His head faced the bathroom door, and I forced myself to act. Taking my phone off the nightstand the activated video feature recorded several seconds of Britto pleasuring himself. It occurred to me the recording would be able to prove that I hadn't participated or interacted with him in any way.

Unable to stomach watching his perverted display for another moment, I stopped recording and put the phone in my pocket. Before I could think what to do next, Britto reached out and grabbed my hand. He yanked me closer to the bed and shoved my hand down between his spread legs, right up against the crack of his ass.

I snatched my hand back and made a noise in my throat that sounded like a cross between a drowning man's gurgle and the frightened whimper of a small child. Then the smell hit me. The same thing I'd detected when we'd first entered the cabin, only a million times stronger. The horrible stench seemed to coat my entire hand.

"Ew! You stink!"

I closed my eyes and snapped my mouth shut. I knew I'd spoken those words, and yet, the words I'd just used to express my disgust weren't ones I would pick, and the tone of my voice even sounded different…younger, much younger… Like a scared little boy, trapped in a situation he couldn't control. *Ew?* Where the hell had that come from? Why didn't I tell him to leave me the fuck alone? Call him a stank-ass bastard who smelled like shit? As I tried to figure out what the heck was going on with me, Britto sat up.

"Oh, I stink?" he said. "You want me to take a shower?" in his distinctive Brazilian accent.

Without waiting for an answer, he clambored off the bed and stumbled toward the bathroom.

Immediately, I saw my route of escape unfold. Britto left the door open, which meant I couldn't get out without closing the bathroom door. Most likely he left the door that way to block me from leaving, but I figured he'd get into the shower soon, and l while I waited, I took the opportunity to go out to the balcony and grab my shirt and put it on. Without any lighting on the balcony, it proved difficult to find my shirt seeming to be a time-consuming task. As I found my shirt I hear Britto exclaim "What are you doing?" Quickly pulling my shirt on, I walked back into the cabin now fully dressed, and grabbed my water bottle and jacket; I was ready to leave. As I reached the door, Britto stumbled out of the bathroom and carelessly used his body to create a barrier between me and the two doors.

"Where are you going?" he asked.

"I need to leave," I said.

He leaned his upper body partway into the bathroom and added more soap to the washcloth in his hand. This allowed him to continue blocking the door while he gave himself a sponge bath.

In that moment, the truth hit me. All the events that had led me to Britto's room had been intentional. A total setup. I had a choice to make, and I had to preserve my credibility and preserve my life. Being in that room awoke something inside me I never knew existed. With my fight-or-flight response stripped away, all I had left was a desire to survive.

"I want to leave," I told him. "I don't want to stay here with you."

Britto pointed toward the bed. "Oh, come on, Shawn, just sit down with me for a few minutes. It'll be fun; I promise."

I shook my head, exasperated over the man's refusal to listen and his seeming inability to take no for an answer. "I'm not staying. Please step aside so I can leave."

I started to move past him, and he grabbed me, one hand on my arm and the other at my waist.

"Please stop. I just want to be your friend." My voice sounded odd, as if it were coming from somewhere outside of my body.

Britto turned his naked body and pressed his buttocks against my groin.

"No!" I told him and tried to jerk away from his disgusting touch.

Britto stood and grabbed my arm, and we began to struggle—me in an attempt to break his hold and flee, while he tried to guide me toward the bed.

"No, no, no, no, no, no, no!" The word left my mouth more times than I exhaled. Then to my horror, I tripped over the shoes he'd kicked off and left in the middle of the floor earlier. Retreating backward from his naked body as he pulls my arms I stumbled and fell onto the bed. Before I could get up, Britto climbed on top of me and pinned me down, his naked body pressed against me.

I lay there in stunned silence for several seconds, my mind blank. Britto shifted his weight as if he was making himself comfortable, settling in for the duration, and his movement jump-started my thoughts. How was I going to get him off me without physically hurting him? How would I stop him from doing whatever he wanted to do while he had me pinned on the bed? He could—

No! I didn't allow myself to finish the thought. "No!" I said, speaking as forcefully as I could. "No!"

I fought back tears as I forced out the word over and over.

"No. No. No. No. No. No. No." I repeated it like a mantra, but Britto either didn't hear or didn't care.

He forced his legs between mine and tried to intertwine our limbs.

"No!" I continued to shout with conviction.

I tried to reach back and shove him off, but he grabbed my wrist and pinned my arm to the bed.

"No!" I forced the word past the tightness in my throat. "I don't want to be here. I don't want to do this. I just want to go back to my room."

Britto lifted some of his weight off me, and I attempted to roll away from him. The position didn't really get any better, since he was still on top of me and I still couldn't get away from him. I felt inclined to face my attacker.

Without moving around too much—the last thing I wanted was to rub against him and have him get the wrong idea—I tried to get up. Britto pressed down harder, using his weight to keep me in place.

"Please fuck me, Shawn," he slurred in his thick accent.

I tried to maintain my composure, but deep down, I feared this could end badly for me. On the edge of hysteria, I began to laugh.

"I'm not like that," I told him. "I just want to be your friend." I laughed again, thinking I could fool myself into believing everything was okay. I tried to force the corners of my lips upward, but my face felt stiff, like a plastic mask. Time seemed to stand still in a bizarre and painful way as the two of us stared each other down. As I looked into his dark, empty eyes, I realized the man did not care about consent.

I felt trapped, scared, and helpless. I *was* trapped and scared and helpless. I couldn't fully process what was happening to me, what he was trying to make me do. The room started spinning, and the walls were closing in.

Dark thoughts crept into my head, and I considered what might have happened if I had shoved this sexual predator over the railing when he'd followed me out to the balcony. I could literally see myself pushing him away and then shoving him harder so he flew backward, teetered on the top rail for a moment, then plunged over and down. The scene played out in my mind like a movie, along with the emotions that went with it—my shock and anger, then a deep sense of satisfaction as I watched him fall. And terror filled me. My life flashed before my eyes as I considered the consequences of such an act.

From the moment he'd first touched me on the balcony, I'd known starting a fight with Britto was a bad idea. If I hurt him, either accidentally or purposely, I could find myself in a world of trouble. The esteemed Romero Britto had fame and money—lots and lots of money—in his favor, and all I had was my word. If anything was to happen to the star guest artist while we were together in his room, all eyes would turn on me, and I'd be under immediate scrutiny. I was trapped, and I had too much to lose. I couldn't risk allowing one anger-driven decision to erase my future, but at that moment, after all I'd endured so far, I wished I would have.

"Will you please get off me?" I asked him again.

Again, he refused. He kept moving his lower body, rubbing against me, and the pressure of his dick on my thigh made me sick. Once more, I doubted my decision to stay, and then immediately I followed up with what might happen if I forced him off and he got hurt. These circular, useless thoughts kept swirling in my head, making me dizzy and even more confused.

"Get off me!" I said, trying to be a little more forceful.

"Have you ever sucked a guy's nipple?" he responded. "You are going to love it, Shawn." He held the sides of my face by my cheeks and ears and tried to force my mouth to his chest. He put a hand on the back of my head and pushed my face toward his chest until my mouth was touching him, all the while coaxing and ordering and cajoling me to suck his nipples.

I kept turning my face away and pulling back, while I repeatedly told him no, and finally, after about twenty or more attempts, he gave up.

For a moment, I felt a surge of relief. He'd let me up now…let me leave. Everything was going to be okay.

He slid his body down, and I expected we'd both get up, but when we were level with each other's eyes, our faces inches apart, he paused. I sensed what was coming an instant before it happened and tried to turn my head, but Britto grabbed my chin, leaned down, and forced his tongue into my mouth. He pressed his dick against me again, harder this time. Too shocked to react, I froze until finally, after what felt like years, he pulled back.

"Please stop." Somehow, I managed to speak past the fear that had closed up my throat. "Let's just be friends, okay? Please…oh, God, please let me go." As he continued to hold onto my wrist attempting to pull me closer to him I asked him, "You're famous. Why me? You just spoke at our meet and greet, telling us about all the famous people you hang out with. Such as the Bush family, and you mentioned that you travel twice a year to London to hang out with Prince Charles. You also mentioned that you have painted more U. S. Presidents than any other artist in the world. Why me?"

I'd finally been reduced to begging, and my humiliation felt complete. But Britto acted as if I hadn't said a word. He continued to attempt to force his tongue into my mouth, only letting up to take a breath and then suffocating me again with the weight of his body and the force of his mouth and face on mine. I couldn't move. I imagined being buried alive felt a lot like being trapped under this two-hundred-pound man.

He began saying vulgar and sometimes nonsensical things in between attempting to force his tongue down my throat.

"Will you kiss my dick?"

"Can I cum all over your face?"

"I want you on top of me—just for a little bit. I want to feel you on top of me."

I answered him with the same words I'd been saying since he came up behind me on the balcony.

"I just want to be your friend."

"Get off me."

"I want to leave. Let me go."

He smiled and reached beneath me, trying to grab hold of my buttocks.

"Stop!" My voice sounded sharp as broken glass.

He pulled his hands back and shrugged. "Fine, then how about you grab hold of my ass?" "We're buddies," I said, "and that's all. Please, please stop."

"We're going be lovers, you know?" Britto said, sliding his tongue down my cheek. "You're so handsome, Shawn. I want you to be my boyfriend."

The feel of his saliva on my face and the smell of his stale-alcohol-tinged breath made my stomach heave.

I'm going to puke. I closed my eyes and drew a couple of long, slow breaths. I couldn't escape the torture, and I started to pray silently, asking God for help, asking Him to intervene.

Dear Lord, this is the worst moment of my life.

The moment the thought was fully formed, images began flooding my head. I recognized myself as a child, and I saw the house my family lived in when I was nine years old. I even recalled the address—300 Independence Circle in Brooksville, Florida—and I saw…I *remembered* what happened to me there. Events so vile and terrifying, my brain had locked those memories away, never to be recalled until this moment.

What Britto was doing, the nature of his attack had shocked my mind into revealing these long-repressed memories of abuse. I recalled the house we lived in and the one across the street. I remembered the man who lived there; his name was David, and when my mom had to work late some nights, she'd send me over to stay with him until she got home. And in vivid, full-color detail, I saw everything David made me do. As a nine-year-old little boy, I'd been forced to touch David's penis and perform oral sex on him. The abuse went on for years until we finally moved away from the house on Independence Circle.

As these images filled my mind, I shuddered, my heart aching for the child I used to be and my anger building over the abuse that little boy had gone through. But I also began to think a little more clearly. Things began to make more sense in terms of my response to Britto's advances. My inability to take decisive action, my feeble attempts to get away…everything tied into the things I'd endured as a child. Even though I hadn't realized it, Britto's actions had thrown me right back into the 1970s, and I'd experienced all the same emotions I'd had as a child. Terror and a sense of helplessness guided my responses.

As I sorted all this out in my head, Britto shifted on top of me and began to stroke himself.

Once again, I asked him to stop, please just stop, but I barely recognized the sound of my own voice. I seriously began to think I might lose my sanity. I had objected to this man's advances for what felt like hours, as he covered me in his alcohol-tainted spit and body odor.

Above me, Britto moved his hips and moaned, and something inside me snapped.

Filled with newfound strength and courage--the consequences be damned—I shoved Britto up and off me as I slid out from beneath him. I got up quickly and turned to face him. I could tell by the look in his eyes that this first truly aggressive act on my part had startled him. Maybe it had even caused him to think about what he'd been doing.

I turned away and went to the door, but when I grasped the knob, I paused.

"Shawn," he mumbled from behind me.

One word and all the doubts and conflicting thoughts I'd had all evening came rushing back. If I left now, would he try to retaliate? If he thought I might report what had happened, he might try to file a report against me first. If he said I'd come to his room and attacked him, it would be my word against his.

I released a deep sigh and turned. I would stay for just a little while longer, make small talk to reassure myself—and him—that what had happened wouldn't go beyond this room, and all I wanted was to leave.

I went back over to the bed and sat on the edge, ready to bolt if he so much as even leaned in my direction. In the friendliest tone I could muster, I talked to him about his itinerary for the next few days. I pretended to be engaged, and I think I managed to fool him into believing we were cool. After a few minutes of inane chit-chat, I decided it was safe to leave. He didn't seem angry…in fact, his eyes had started to close, so I got up to leave.

I opened the cabin door, but before I stepped out, I turned back. I had to say something in my defense.

"How many men have you tried to seduce like this?" I asked. "You need to understand when a person says no, it means no. I asked you to stop repeatedly, saying No again and again but you acted like you didn't even hear me…"

Britto was silent for a moment, but finally, he shrugged. "Nobody, I swear on my mother's life." He didn't even look at me. His eyes were closed, and he seemed ready to pass out. "I just want you as my boyfriend."

I left Britto's cabin to the sound of his snoring as the door clicked behind me.

HERBERT "SHAWN" MILLER

' # Chapter 4

TO THIS DAY, I don't remember walking back to my room that early morning. I don't remember how my body functioned well enough to carry me there. Numb from head to toe, my legs like rubber, I stopped at my cabin door, slid my key into the lock, and stepped inside. The sound of my wife snoring greeted me, a comforting and familiar sound, but when the door clicked shut behind me, the terrible odor of Romero Britto flooded my senses. The realistic part of my brain realized he wasn't right there with me, but the horrible stench of his dirty ass overwhelmed all rational thought. I could smell him all around me as if his body odor filled my pores. Immediately, I went into the bathroom, and after I disrobed, I climbed into the shower and turned on the water, adjusting the temperature as hot as it would go. Before I realized it, I had curled into a fetal position on the shower stall floor. Although my body had seemed to give out, at least for the moment, my brain kept throwing out one painful thought after another.

What was I going to do now? The last few hours hadn't felt real. How could this have happened to me? I sat in the shower for over four hours that early morning with the hot water beating down from overhead. I wanted to wash away the stain of Britto's touch from my skin and wished I could rinse the memories from my mind, too. Could I live the rest of my life with the images of what happened to me burned into my brain, where they could pop up at any moment? Would that be a life worth living? My mind wandered to a dark place. I've never been suicidal, but as I tried to wash Romero Britto from my thoughts and my skin, I considered hurting myself. No…I wanted to *kill* myself. I wanted to commit suicide. I closed my eyes, and in living color, a horribly detailed plan formed. I pictured wrapping one end of a long white sheet around my neck and tying the other to the railing on the balcony of my cabin room. I watched as I climbed over and balanced on the two inches of decking hundreds of feet above the ocean. I drew a deep breath then slid my feet forward, and my body weight caused me to plunge down toward the water. An instant later, the sheet caught tight, stopping my descent, and my body swung free. The white fabric cut into my throat and stole the last few breaths from my body.

WHY ME?

The vivid scene consumed me, along with the knowledge I'd no longer suffer the ugly, painful memories Britto had cemented inside my head.

I got to my feet and put my face up to the spray. Could I go through with it? I'd done nothing to stop Britto from abusing me. Could I find the courage to put an end to my suffering?

As if to answer those questions, my thoughts turned to my daughters. An image of their smiling faces replaced the plan I'd constructed to harm myself. While I might pull together enough courage to go through with killing myself, I could never hurt my girls.

My daughters needed me. My family needed me. I needed to be strong for them. I could not give up. I would not kill myself. A long list of all the reasons why I needed to stay alive played in my head, and I forced myself to shut off the water and step out of the shower. As I wrapped a towel around my waist, I realized I was on shaky ground. I needed to talk to someone. Fast. I needed space to express these feelings before 1 did something I could not take back.

I grabbed my cell phone off the counter and placed a call to my long-time friend Brian, the chaplain at the Pasco County Sheriff's Office. The phone rang and rang, but no one picked up. I tried to call a few more times before I realized that, while out on the open ocean, I couldn't make calls back to the U.S. My cell phone did not work on the boat, but I had Wi-Fi access in my room. I brought up the FaceTime app, and using the ship's wi-fi, I made a video call to the chaplain's wife, since she had an iPhone. As the call rang, I prayed desperately for someone to pick up. I really needed to talk. I needed to let these emotions out in a way that wouldn't cause more harm. Finally, his wife came into view, and I asked to speak to Brian. She didn't ask any questions, thank goodness, and a second later, Brian came on the phone. I told him what had happened to me, how Britto had lured me to his room and then attacked me, the words tumbling out as fast as I could say them. Brian sat and listened to everything I had to say.

God, it felt good to be heard. To share the burden of what had happened with someone else.

"Are you okay?" he asked when I finished.

I didn't know how to answer him. I hadn't bothered to ask myself that question, and now, I didn't know how to feel. Although I knew how to feel about the situation I'd been forced into, I didn't know if I was okay or if the random thoughts I'd had since making my escape were normal. My emotions were in turmoil, ranging from wishing I was dead to wishing Britto was dead. Like a movie, the abuse I'd suffered—both recent and in the past—played in my head. How did I cope with all that? Did I even want to? I didn't know, and I told Brian as much.

"Well, are you thinking about hurting yourself?" he asked.

I decided on complete transparency. I told him about the vivid plan I'd put together while I was in the shower.

"Up until now, I never even considered suicide. Never…" I told him after describing how I'd planned to hang myself. "The only thing that stopped me today was my love for my daughters. I couldn't leave them. Thoughts of those girls are the only things that are helping me maintain my composure and keep a clear head."

"That's good to hear," Brian said. "Make sure you keep those girls in mind."

Feeling a little better after sharing my burden with a good friend, I wrapped up the conversation. "Thanks for talking to me, and don't worry; I think I'll be okay."

"Have you talked to Kelly about this?" he asked.

"No!" How could I wake my wife and tell her what had happened to me? Did she need to know? Was there any point in upsetting her?"

"You really need to let her in on this. She's a good, strong woman; let her help you."

I hesitated, but Brian was right. Kelly would stand by me and help in any way, even if that just meant listening when I needed to talk.

I agreed to talk to my wife, and Brian told me to call him any time, day or night, if I needed anything. Then he put on his chaplain hat and ended our conversation with a short prayer.

After I terminated the FaceTime call, I lifted my head. I couldn't just sit there in the bathroom all day. I needed to talk to my wife about the filthy secret I'd been trying to wash from my consciousness for the last several hours, but I wasn't ready.

Ironically, even though a part of me realized I was acting crazy, I got back into the shower because it was the only place I felt somewhat sane. I stood under the water for a while and let a numbness come over me before I heard noises coming from the main cabin. My wife was awake... She stepped into the small cabin bathroom to tell me good morning.

"Is something wrong?" she asked.

How well she knew me—even separated by the glass shower door and all the built up steam, she sensed something about me was off.

"No. Just taking a nice, long shower," I told her, forcing an upbeat tone.

Kelly didn't speak for a few seconds, and I hoped she wouldn't pursue her suspicions.

"Well, do you want me to wait for you, and we can go down to breakfast together?"

My insides recoiled at the thought. All those people... I couldn't face them. What if Britto had talked? News like that spread like wildfire, and I imagined him twisting the facts to suit his own agenda. Although I know now I was the victim of an heinous sexual assault, at that time I felt as if I were branded with a large scarlet letter A.

"No, thanks." I forced the words past the sick lump in my throat. "I'm going to be a little while. You go ahead and enjoy your breakfast."

Again, she took a while to answer, and rather than face any further questions, I tried to pull myself together enough to reassure her.

"Go. Go, enjoy your breakfast" I poked my head out of the shower and offered her a smile.

She nodded, shrugged, then went off to the dining hall. The heavy cabin door clicked closed behind her.

no one should EVER....

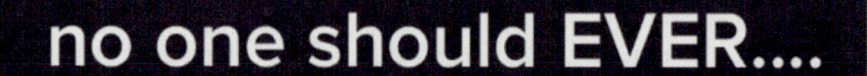

he artist Romero Britto breaks he silence by painting himself s a victim and describing ontroversy as 'fake news'

archyde 4 months a

This isn't fake news! photos and videos are available!

he Brazilian painter Romero Britto, involved in

Chapter 5

WHEN MY WIFE returned from her morning meal, I was still in the shower. She poked her head in and asked if I needed anything.

I needed to tell her now. No one spends hours in the shower. She had to know something was up. I turned the metal handle to shut off the stream of water and opened the shower door. Instead of getting out, however, I pressed my forehead against the cool shower stall wall. Without looking at her, I started talking.

As I told my wife about how Romero Britto sexually assaulted me and held me captive for hours, tears clogged the back of my throat.

Telling Kelly caused a damn to break inside. Rather than simply saying the words and explaining events as if they'd happened to someone else, I finally confronted the detailed reality of what had been done to me. I broke down, slipping to the floor of the stall as the tears made their escape and ran down my cheeks.

I couldn't stop sobbing, could barely catch my breath. Kelly leaned forward from her perch on the toilet and wrapped her arms around me.

"It'll be okay." Her voice cracked. "Start from the beginning and tell me everything. I promise it'll be okay. I'll help you."

We cried together as I told her about every single thing that had transpired the night before. I didn't try to sugarcoat anything or spare myself any embarrassment. We talked for a little over an hour, and my wife confessed that she'd known something was wrong, but she didn't know what.

When I finished talking, Kelly sat back on the toilet and wiped the tears from her face.

My entire body ached, inside and out. I got to my feet, and although I felt a little better after talking to her, I really needed some time alone. When I opened my mouth to ask her if she would mind if I went to lie down by myself for a while, Kelly shook her head.

"It's okay," she said. "I understand. I'll get out of here and give you some peace."

She left our cabin and left me with my thoughts. I was thankful for the solitude.

I had just enough energy to climb into bed.

WHY ME?

Although I felt an innate need to process my emotions, I couldn't form a coherent thought. I lay under the blanket for hours, forcing back the raging mixed emotions until I felt numb. A few times, I did rouse myself from that comatose-like state long enough for my feet to carry me back into the shower. The horrible smell I'd encountered in Britto's room haunted me. It woke me from my sleep many times throughout that day and night. Each time, I'd climb right back in under the shower and lather myself from head to toe. But no matter how many times I tried to wash the stench from my skin, I couldn't escape it.

I stayed in this insane cycle for two days—bed, shower, bed, shower, bed, shower. I slept some of the time, but for most of those hours, I lay there awake.

My thoughts consumed me and pushed me to feel nothing. After two days of being too weak to leave the cabin, I started going a little stir crazy. The walls were starting to close in on me.

The next morning, I rose from the bed before the sun came up. To escape the claustrophobia, I left the cabin and took the elevator to the upper deck. I put on my headphones, put on my music app, and walked the deck for over three hours. Round and round I went in one continuous circle. The music in my ears helped to calm my racing thoughts. The breeze on my face gave me the same sense of security the shower did. I felt a tiny bit of hope as the sun came up that I'd make it through another day.

The ship slowly started to buzz with the sounds made by other early risers. My morning walk ended as fellow cruisers carried their breakfast trays to unoccupied tables along the deck. I sat at a table stared aimlessly into the distance for a bit and then watched the vacationers around me. *How nice they must feel...still enjoying this trip.* No one else on the deck seemed to be experiencing what I was experiencing; no one else acted as if their entire life had been turned upside down while they traveled aboard the Norwegian Encore.

I summoned one of the servers working on the dining deck and asked for a pen and a piece of paper. At that moment, watching everyone else around me carry on normally and uninterrupted, I decided I needed to get my thoughts out of my head and onto paper. Just as I began to write, Kelly called me via FaceTime video.

"Hi! Where are you?" she asked.

"Up on the dining deck," I told her. "After two days, I needed to get out of that room."

"That's wonderful," she said in a low voice. "I'll come up, and we can have breakfast together."

She sounded hopeful yet restrained. While I waited, I wrote my thoughts down on the small notepad-sized pieces of paper the crewmember had given me. My thoughts were scrambled and erratic, but I wrote anyway. I scribbled quickly and fervently, determined not to miss a single detail as I documented everything I knew in that moment. As I finished, my wife approached the table carrying two plates. She smiled at me, and I imagine she was happy to see me out of bed.

She set one of the plates on the table in front of me, and for for the first time in forty-eight hours, I decided to try to eat. I grabbed a forkful of food and inched it toward my lips, but the smell made my stomach turn.

Overcome by exhaustion, I set down the fork and pushed away the plate. I hadn't eaten or slept well in two days, and without food or sleep, the next few days on the boat would only get harder for me. I couldn't escape the feeling of helplessness.

I watched my wife eat her breakfast as some of the other invited VIP art buyers we met at the beginning of our excursion came over to our table.

Wearing a wide smile, one of the women said, "Where have you guys been? Are you okay?"

"You all have missed at least two of our VIP outings; what's up?" her friend added.

They seemed concerned and genuinely curious, as well as happy to see us, while I couldn't summon more of a response than a tremulous smile. Luckily, my wife was there to lend her support.

"A family friend passed away," she explained. "We just got word a few days ago."

WHY ME?

The two women expressed their condolences and understanding, before walking farther down the deck to another table where they stopped to greet other fellow travelers.

Kelly's explanation had worked. She smiled at me then returned to eating her breakfast, but I still felt like I was drowning. We couldn't tell anyone about what had happened a few nights before. I was too afraid. Afraid of what could happen, afraid of being pitted against Romero Britto, afraid of not being believed… Of course, I had evidence in the form of the recording on my cellphone, but while we were still on the boat, would that be enough to prove I wasn't lying? Fear led to suspicion. How would this story play out if something were to happen to my phone? I made a mental note to put my phone in the safe in our room as soon as we got back to our cabin.

When Kelly finished eating, we went back to our room. I told her my idea about stashing my phone in the safe, and she agreed. That way, we'd be sure no one could tamper with the evidence, and I wouldn't risk dropping my cell in the ocean and losing everything.

I locked my device in the safe, as Kelly read the itinerary for the day aloud.

"Now that you're up and about, it's important for you to keep up that momentum," she said. "There's another VIP art showing tonight. Do you want to go?"

I thought about it a couple minutes then nodded. I didn't want to keep hiding, and there were a lot of great artists on this ship. Maybe we could find one who painted pieces we could use to replace Britto's.

During the first few art showings at the beginning of the trip, we'd made an impression on some of the other guests. When we arrived at the large room where that evening's show was being held, the few friends we made early on came over to us and asked where we had disappeared to and if everything was okay. We explained, as we did up on the dining deck, that a close friend of ours had died.

Although my wife did most of the talking, the guilt I felt about lying to these people compounded my distress. My hands started to shake, and the moment we were standing by ourselves again, Kelly touched my arm.

"Are you okay?" she asked. "Do you want to leave?"

I shook my head and stuffed my hands into my pockets. "No. I'll be alright."

I would make it to the end of that auction if it killed me.

The auctioneer called for everyone's attention, and Kelly and I walked toward the front so we could have a good view of the artwork. Over the course of the next few hours, the auctioneer showed pieces by Duaiv, Peter Max…and Romero Britto.

I wasn't at all surprised to discover my newfound distaste for Britto's work. Every piece reminded me of the man behind the art, and I was disgusted. I wanted to turn away. Being near his paintings was nearly as bad as being in the same room with the man, and I began to feel trapped.

Thankfully, the auctioneer moved on to the next artist's work, and I bid on an electric painting of a French bulldog by Mr. Duaiv. Kelly and I had recently bought a French bulldog for our youngest daughter Jayla. Duaiv had painted this Frenchie puppy in bright pink and other neon colors—the perfect piece of art for our family. The dog in the painting looked identical to our dog Stitch.

After we won the auction on that piece, Mr. Duaiv came over and signed the painting and then posed for a photo with us. As we smiled for the camera, I glanced over toward the entrance. Jordan had just entered the gallery. Even from a distance, I noticed the abnormal, bright-red color of his face. As he came closer, I smelled the alcohol seeping from his pores. I smiled at him, despite the flashback that odor caused.

"You reek of booze," I told him then laughed. "And why is your face so red?"

"Long night drinking!" he said.

My stomach flipped. What was nothing more than lighthearted fun for him had turned my life upside down. I shook my head and walked away, no longer able to hide my disgust and distress. Jordan and his associates had left Katherine and Britto at the bar, despite the fact they'd both had far too much to drink. Anger built inside me.

WHY ME?

Romero Britto needed to be held accountable for his actions, and ultimately, he was to blame. No one knew that better than I did. But in that moment—and even now if I had the opportunity—I wanted to ask Park West representatives why they had left Britto, an artist who makes them millions of dollars per year, subject to such scandal? Why would they invite a man aboard to represent their company, and then leave him alone in the state he had been in? Many Park West associates had been there when Britto was out-of-his-mind drunk. Why didn't anybody try to stop things from getting out of hand? And my million-dollar question—why was I the only one there that night who stepped up and offered to help?

HERBERT "SHAWN" MILLER

Chapter 6

THE EMOTIONAL TOLL of being on the same ship as my attacker began to get to me more than I expected it would. The last few days onboard were nearly unbearable. My wife and I were ready to get back home. As we neared port in Puerto Rico, I decided to reach out to Britto. After so many exhausting days and nearly sleepless nights, I wanted an apology. As the ship pulled close to the island, I stood on my balcony. Britto would be getting off the boat for good in Puerto Rico, and this felt like the safest time to call him. As everyone else left the boat to take part in all the fun-filled island excursions, Kelly and I stayed behind. I used the number Britto put into my phone the night he'd attacked me, and I called him. After a few rings he answered. The sound of his breathing filled my ear, along with the buzz of hundreds of people walking on the ship's docking area.

I stood on my balcony and spoke into the mouthpiece. "Hey, man, this is Shawn."

He answered in his thick, Brazilian accent. "Shawn? How do I know you, Shawn?"

Surprisingly enough, his question brought me a bit of relief. "I'm the guy who helped you and Katherine get back to your rooms the other night."

"Really? I don't recall that, and I'm sorry, but I don't remember you." He sounded genuinely confused and sincere.

The sense of relief grew. If Britto didn't remember anything about that night, then maybe he truly hadn't been lucid enough to know he was assaulting me. Maybe it was all a big misunderstanding. Maybe he had truly been too drunk out of his mind. This was the closure I had needed. I could move past those events if he hadn't known what he was doing…if he had simply made a mistake.

"Oh, hey, Shawn?" Britto said. "Do you still have my glasses?"

I think my heart stopped, and I literally quit breathing for a moment. I couldn't believe my ears, and I quickly hit the button on my cell to disconnect the call. My thoughts ran rampant. The man held me hostage for hours, had touched and fondled me against my wishes. He was acting as if he didn't remember me, and yet, he recalled giving me his glasses. I was so angry, disappointed, and distraught. The tears began rolling down my face again as I stood on the balcony. Romero Britto knew exactly who I was, and he remembered every single thing he'd done that night. I started gagging and had to gulp air to calm my rolling stomach. I couldn't excuse his actions. There was no easy way out, and I wouldn't be getting the closure I so desperately needed.

The next day, nothing had improved. If anything, they may have gotten a little worse. Although I had the comfort of knowing I wouldn't run into Britto because he'd gotten off the ship and stayed in Puerto Rico, Kelly and I still had another hurdle to overcome. During the first few nights onboard, before the assault, she and I placed winning bids on over sixty-thousand dollars' worth of art. We'd been so excited to know we'd be taking those paintings home with us…but now? Britto had painted the majority of them, and no way would Kelly or I lend our support or give another penny of our hard-earned money to that monster. We needed to figure out a way tell them we couldn't be finalizing our purchases on those pieces—a way that didn't involve me telling the Park West associates what occurred on the morning of December 10.

With all auctions, a buyer bids on a piece that catches his or her eye, and if they win the bid, they wait for a Park West associate to come over with an appointment card. On the card the associate writes out a date, time, and place indicating when the buyer is to return to sort out the final financial details before the purchase is set in stone. A lot of pieces in our collection came from Park West, and this was a process we'd gone through many times. Our appointment had been set for one of the last few days aboard the ship, which happened to be the day after my useless and insulting conversation with Britto.

That night, Kelly and I walked down to the art gallery. After talking things over, we'd decided to pay for some of the art we had won, and we had created a story to explain why we couldn't purchase the art we had no intentions of ever allowing into our home.

But when we stepped through the door into the gallery, we stopped cold. Instead of dealing with each buyer privately and separately, they'd set up a row of tables. An auctioneer sat on one side of each table, and their buyers sat across from them. The uncomfortable setup would allow us to hear other buyers' financial and personal information, and they'd be able to hear ours. Only the fact we'd made many purchases with Park West and had confidence in their discretion caused us to go through with our appointment. Looking back now, I believe we should have recognized this unusual method of completing the sales as a red flag.

We sat at one of the folding tables in the row. The woman collecting our information introduced herself as Lisa, and our encounter with her started off pleasantly.

Feeling hopeful we'd get this overwith quickly and amicably, I sat forward. "Lisa," I began, speaking low so my voice didn't carry beyond our little card table. "I need to apologize. Unfortunately, my wife and I won't be able to purchase all the paintings we won…"

Her bright smile disappeared, and her dark brows lowered. "Excuse me? What do you mean you won't be able to purchase them all?"

Her attitude and tone of voice couldn't have been frostier. "Very upset" didn't begin to describe her reaction. Her hands were shaking as she shuffled through a stack of papers on the table in front of her.

Sucking in a deep breath, I continued. "I'm very sorry, but shortly after the first few auctions, we learned of the death of a dear family friend."

"Yes," Kelly put in. "That's why we weren't at any of the events for several days." She put her hand on my arm. "My husband and I were shocked and distraught."

Lisa turned her cool stare toward Kelly but didn't respond. You would have thought we were a couple art thieves, and not two longtime Park West patrons who'd spent a great deal of money with them.

"We aren't looking for sympathy," I said, pushing forward. "However, our decision is final. Kelly and I have decided to donate the funds we would have spent on the other artwork to our friend's family, which will be put toward his funeral expenses and help to support his family during this very difficult time. We can't take the Peter Max or any of the pieces by Romero Britto, but we would still like to buy the two paintings by Duaiv."

Lisa looked back and forth between my wife and me, before shaking her head and rifling through the papers again, as if she were looking for something. My guess was that she didn't have the courage to look us in the eyes and lie.

"I'm sorry," she said, "but that's unacceptable. We've already packaged and sent the artwork to the home address we have for you in our file." Finally, she looked up. "Besides, by bidding, you're agreeing to make the purchase. It's like a contract, and I'm afraid we can't allow you to renege on these purchases."

I shifted in my seat, and my irritation with the woman almost got the better of me, but I managed to keep calm. Kelly, on the other hand, tends to cry when she's really angry, and this time was no exception. As Park West VIP members, we'd been dealing with the gallery for years and had paid them hundreds of thousands of dollars for artwork, and we'd never been treated with such disrespect.

"Well, that's great," Kelly said, snatching a tissue from her purse and dabbing at her eyes. "Then I guess we need to thank you for the free art, because we aren't signing anything or paying for anything other than the two pieces my husband told you we want."

"Ma'am, if you didn't want the paintings, you shouldn't have placed bids on them. There are other people who could have and would have loved to own all those beautiful pieces. You've deprived them of that opportunity." Lisa took a form from the stack of papers and picked up a pen. "As I said, you agreed to make these purchases… all of them. Now, shall we go ahead and finish up here?"

Lisa's condescending tone made my blood boil. And she really thought she was going to bully us into buying pieces of art we no longer wanted. Her pushiness grated on my nerves, and I felt a little like I was dealing with a used car salesman.

"I'd like to speak to someone else, please. Someone who's in a higher position of authority with the gallery," I finally said.

"Why in the hell do you need to speak with someone else?" Lisa asked. "I've just explained our policy on these things. Anyone else will tell you the exact same damn thing!"

I nearly lost it then. I could not believe she was sitting there swearing and refusing to allow us to talk to anyone else. Especially when I knew for a fact she was lying, and I believed another auctioneer or a gallery sales manager could resolve this for us quickly.

Lisa sat like a rock in her chair, refusing my request, and I began to wonder if we should just walk out.

"Is there a problem?" One of the other auctioneers who'd been seated a couple tables down came over to stand beside Lisa. He looked at my wife and me and then put a hand on Lisa's shoulder.

"Yes." She looked up at him then pointed across the table in my general direction. "These people say they aren't buying everything they won. I told them they didn't have that choice, and that they'd agreed to make the purchases when they placed their bids."

"Which is a lie!" Kelly said. "This isn't the first or even the tenth time we've done this. I think we're pretty familiar with the process."

"Now you're calling me a liar?" Kelly's voice rose.

The couple at the next table looked in our direction and then began whispering to each other.

"Lisa, why don't you let me handle this, okay?" the other auctioneer said.

He waited for her to get up then took her place in the chair. "Alright, then. Although it's against policy, I suppose we'll have to make an exception in this case."

He slid the blank form in front of him. "Let me write this up, collect your payment information, and you can be on your way."

"I can't believe you're letting them get away with this." Lisa's lip curled, and she scowled at me. "Maybe don't bid on works you don't intend to buy!"

I shook my head and gnawed my bottom lip. I could argue with her, exchange insults, but that would just cause this whole surreal experience to last longer. So, I kept my mouth shut. I wanted out of that room so badly, I wanted to scream.

Lisa stood right behind her chair and continued to make nasty comments.

"We'd like the pieces by Duaiv," I said, "but you need to know, we're never buying another piece of art through Park West again." I paused for a moment, thinking the idea of losing a valuable member might cause at least one of them to change their attitude, but they both stayed quiet. Apparently, neither of them were interested in diffusing the situation.

They helped us sign our deal but continued to make snide, demeaning comments.

When we were finished, neither auctioneer thanked us. Kelly and I got up and started for the door.

"Hey!" Lisa called loud enough for the whole room to hear.

We turned around.

"Just so you know, you two are no longer invited to the VIP Exit Party."

My wife and I laughed and left the gallery. Even before the horrible experience we'd just had with two of their representatives, we'd had no intentions of going to that party. The garbage we'd been through on that boat hadn't exactly put us in the mood to celebrate.

All we wanted to do was make it through another night of crappy sleep and getting off the ship as soon as possible the next morning. We needed to put Norwegian Encore behind us.

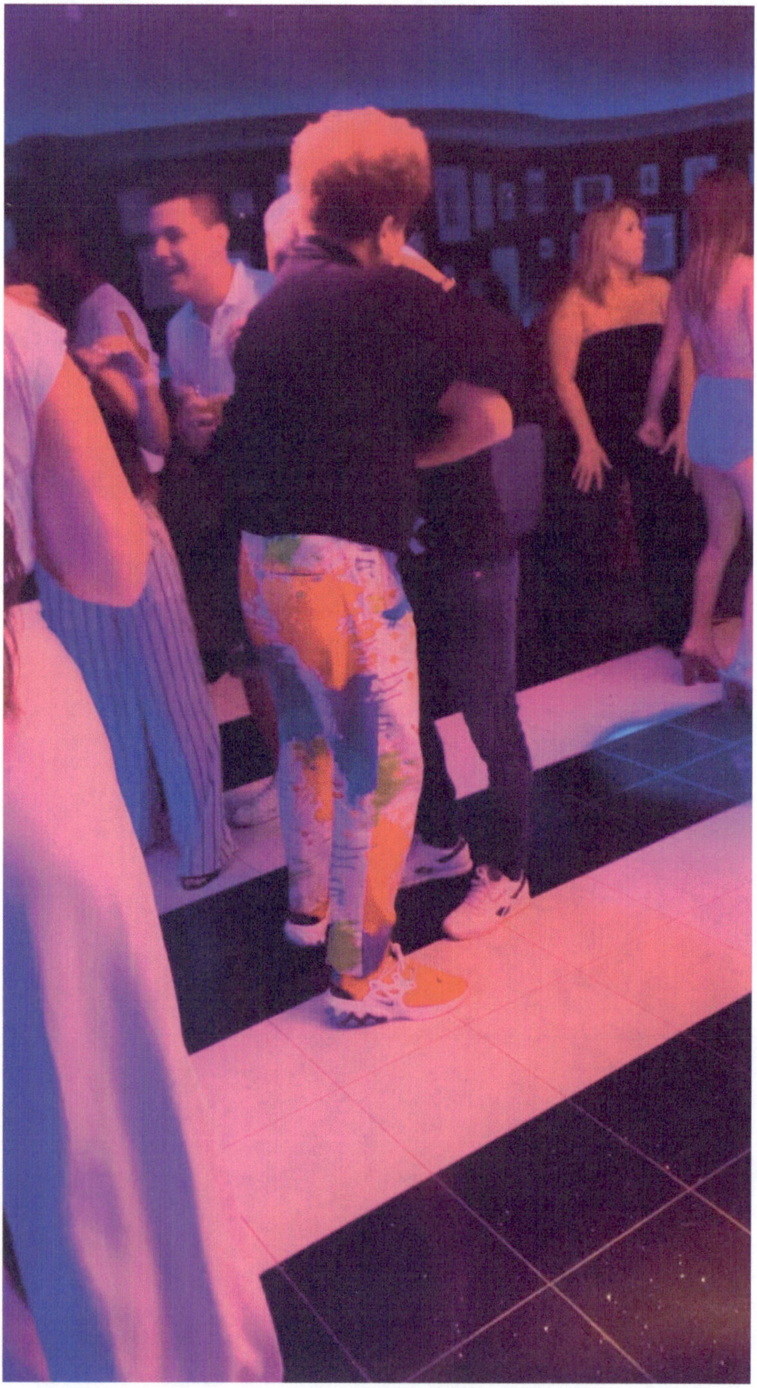

The Aftermath

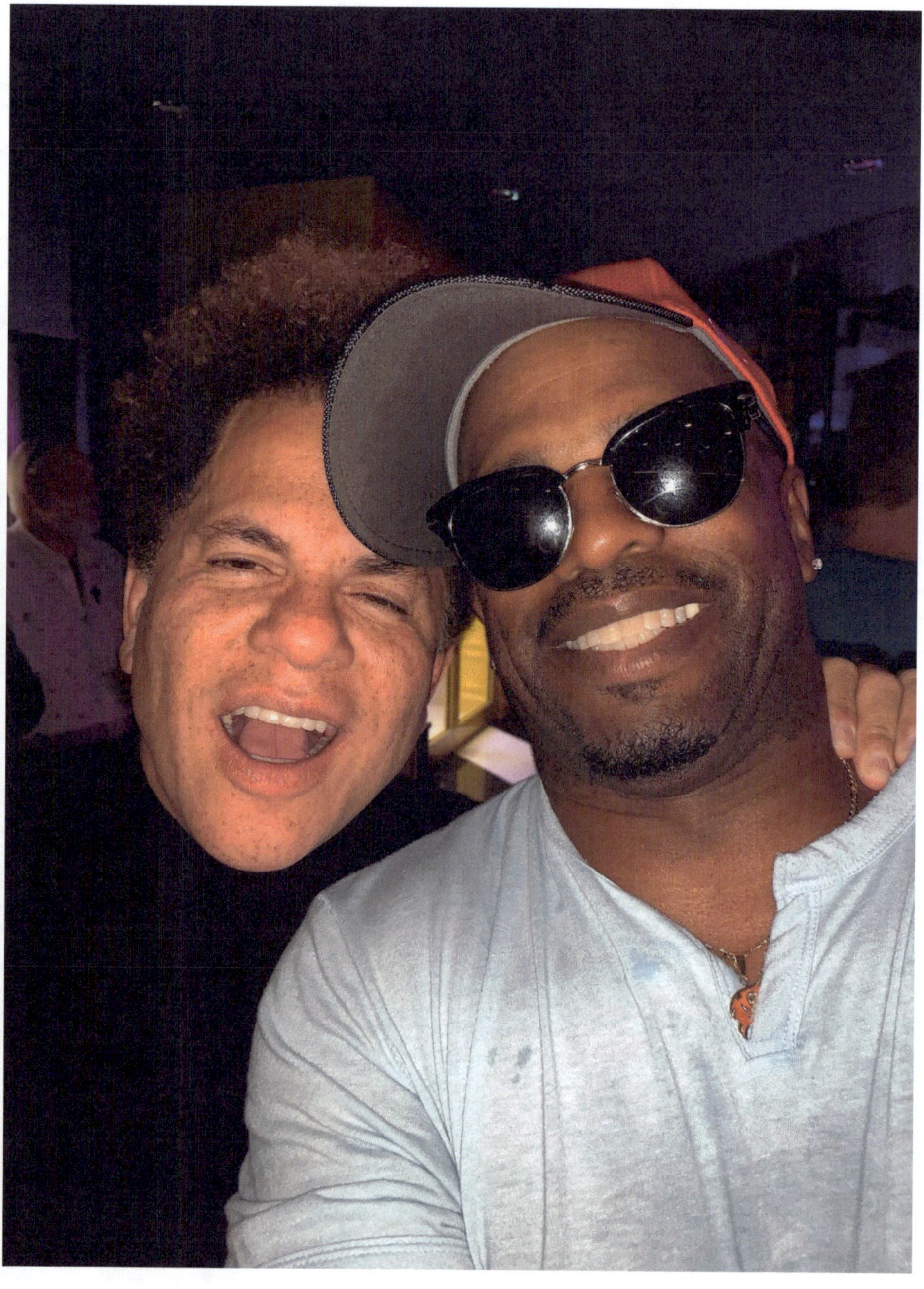

Chapter 7

BEING BACK HOME was a relief, but I didn't feel as free as I'd thought I would. Although I'd left the ship, I hadn't left my troubles behind me. Mentally, I was still trapped.

When Kelly and I walked through our front door, our three daughters were there to greet us with hugs. I let the familiar comfort wash over me, but I was too lost in my own thoughts to contribute to the conversations the four ladies in my house were having.

"Did you guys have fun?"

"Did you meet anyone cool?"

"What did you guys buy?"

"Did you have fun at the auctions?"

"Did you bring us anything?"

One after the other, they peppered us with questions. My daughters were excited to have us home, and I was happy to see their smiling faces, but when they directed their questions toward me, I couldn't respond with more than a few words and showed very little enthusiasm. My mind was everywhere. My thoughts were a jumbled mess. An overwhelming sadness consumed me, making it impossible for me to function as I had before our trip. Romero Britto controlled me in my own home. As much as I wanted to, as much as I *needed* to, I couldn't shake him off.

***

Depression dogged me for days and then weeks. 1 remember my very first breakdown very vividly.

I was driving to one of my twelve rental homes to do a few repairs, and I recall telling myself something wasn't right. My emotional state had deteriorated. No longer depressed but functioning, as I'd been since departing the Norwegian, suddenly, I'd started spiraling downward. Although plagued by incredible sadness, despite the beautiful morning, I determined I'd push through. I had a lot of work to finish that day.

I made it to my property and got started on the renovations I had to do. I planned on painting the interior—walls, doors, trim… even the ceilings. I gathered all my supplies, and just as I applied the trim brush to a wall in the living room, I fell apart. In the blink of an eye and without any warning, my throat closed up, a sob filled my chest, and I began to cry. Not quietly, as I might do if I had more control. This was loud and messy. Snot ran from my nose to join the tears dripping onto my lips and chin. The emotional breakdown went on and on, as if someone had turned a knob and let loose every tear I had ever held back in my lifetime. I struggled to draw a deep breath, to calm myself, but the tears just kept coming. The walls around me started closing in. Soon, I'd be trapped in there, inside a nightmare that started replaying in my head. I'd lost all control, and a tiny, still sane part of my brain told me to call someone. Now. I staggered over to the kitchen counter where I'd set my keys and my phone. I snatched them both up and ran from the house as quickly as my legs would carry me. I had two semi-rational thoughts—get to my car, where I'd be safe, and call my cousin.

My cousin Deborah had been a devout Christian for as long as I could remember, and she was always willing to lend an ear. I climbed into the driver's seat and dailed Deborah's number.

As I began the twelve-minute drive back to my house, the phone started to ring. Thankfully, I knew the route well enough that I didn't have to focus all my attention on the road. Because before I made it to the end of the block, I got lost inside my head, and I was right back in that cabin room. Right back in Britto Romero's filthy clutches. Reliving my very own horror movie, scene by deviant scene. I *saw* him. I *felt* him touch me, and worst of all, I *smelled* him. That nasty, stinky, dirty ass smell. The odor seemed to fill my car, and inside my head, where I was trapped in the moment when Romero Britto forced my hand down to the crack of his stinky, smelly ass, the smell surrounded me. I choked on it, gagged, and then started to cry again.

"Hello? Hello? Are you there?" Deborah's voice broke through my hysteria and pulled me back to the present.

"Oh, thank God." I took a couple big gulps of air and then started talking. The words tumbled out as fast as I could say them in between sobs. I told her everything, all the gory details, and I explained what I'd been thinking and feeling since I'd been attacked.

I even told her about all the hours I'd been spending in the shower, trying to wash off the stomach-churning stench of a man I hadn't even seen in weeks.

Deborah listened quietly. When I finished and finally fell silent, the sound of my cousin crying softly filtered through the phone.

"I am so, so sorry," she said. "No one should ever have to go through something like that. But it'll be okay. *You'll* be okay. You just have to have faith." She paused then asked, "Would you let me say a prayer for you?"

"Yeah." My voice sounded rough, and my throat felt like someone had taken heavy-duty sandpaper to the inside.

Deborah and I talked and prayed until I pulled into my driveway, and then we sat in silence for awhile until I thought I'd recovered enough to make it into the house.

Deborah ended our conversation with another prayer, like she'd put holy bookends around the evil contained in my story in order to contain it. I thanked her and disconnected the call.

I had to gather my strength to shut off the car, get out of my vehicle, and make it in my front door. The ten foot distance felt like a hundred miles...

The experience my mind had put through over roughly the last hour left me feeling drained and dirty. Without thinking I made my way down the hall and into the bathroom. I disrobed and climbed into the shower, and after turning the hot water on full blast, I sank down to sit in the corner of the stall. I stayed there for the remainder of the day as the hot water poured down on me. When the tank ran out of hot, I'd switch over to cold until the hot water tank had a chance to refill. The icy blast of water shocked my system and stung my skin, but I accepted the pain in silence. As if I was doing penance for my sins.

Before I knew it, night had come. Kelly and the girls were due any moment, but I couldn't find the energy or the will to leave my sanctuary. Lukily, Kelly got there first. She found me in the same position I'd been in most of the day. The steam in the room probably told her I'd been in there much longer than I should have been.

WHY ME?

"Come on." Kelly spoke softly and held out her hand. "I'll help you get dressed. The girls will be here any minute."

If I hadn't expected my daughters home, I probably wouldn't have refused Kelly's help and stayed put. But I figured the least I could do was greet them fully clothed.

***

I managed to put on a sweatshirt and sweatpants and take a seat in my recliner in the front room when my lovely young ladies came in the front door. However, I hadn't been able to pull myself up and out of the darkness shrouding my mind.

The girls said hello to me, but I stared past them, hoping they wouldn't spot the pain in my eyes, and nodded. I couldn't form words, let alone muster the strength to put on a brave face and pretend everything was okay.

They accepted my silence and didn't push me to talk. After a quick "I love you, Dad," from each of them, the three girls headed farther into the house, probably to find their mother.

I sat like a lump in that chair for hours. Every so often, one of my family members came down the hall to check on me.

"Do you need anything?" whichever girl who'd come to make sure I was okay would ask.

And every time, I'd mutter, "No, thank you," and force a way-too-polite smile.

Instead of embracing their presence and welcoming their concern, I'd begun to push them away, and that couldn't go on for much longer. I couldn't force my family to tip-toe around me while I grieved the husband, father, and man I had been before Romero Britto stole all my joy and passion for life.

As soon as everyone else had gone to bed, I headed right back into the shower. Standing beneath the spray, I decided I needed professional help if I was going to make it through this tragedy and come out the otherside whole.

***

The next morning, I called my primary physician, and he gave me a referral to a good therapist he said he knew. She even made housecalls, which gave me an idea.

I called the therapist's office and told the woman who answered—the receptionist, I assumed—that I was thinking about seeing the doctor, but I had a few questions first.

Unlike Lisa at Park West, this woman had a kind attitude and the type of quiet patience I'd expect from a preschool teacher. She addressed all my concerns about confidentiality, the types of therapies the doctor used, as well as the types of mental health issues she normally treated. Satisfied with the answers, I paused then said, "I understand the doctor makes housecalls; is that correct?"

"Oh, yes, absolutely. Would you prefer to set up a time for her to come to your home?"

"Actually, no…" I told her. "I was hoping I could make a special request. I know this is probably really unusual, but do you think she'd be willing to meet at a local restaurant? I'll be happy to find a place close to her office so she doesn't have to travel very far."

The receptionist was silent for a moment, then she said, "Well, I don't see why not. I mean, if you're okay talking about private, personal issues in a public place, I think the doctor will be fine accommodating that request. At least for the first session or two."

"That's all I'm asking." I hurried to assure her. "I think I'd feel a lot more comfortable, actually, especially if we meet somewhere I've been to several times. The idea of spilling my guts in an unfamiliar office would probably intimidate me and make me feel as if I'd given up all control. And right now, that's part of my problem. I need to feel as if I'm in control of myself and my environment. I don't like to feel trapped."

"I understand. When and where would you like to meet?" She went on to list several days and times the doctor had open over the next week and a half."

Since I didn't seem to be getting any better, and I probably risked getting worse if I waited very much longer, I chose a time slot for two days from then. While she asked for my name, address, and phone number to enter into their system, I opened the browser app on my cell and found their location. Then, using the address provided online, I checked my maps app to see what restaraunts were close by.

"And how about Denny's?" I asked. "It's only a few blocks away from your office."

"Very good, sir," the receptionist said. "I've set that up for you. Do you have any more questions for me before we hang up?"

I couldn't think of any and figured if I did, I could always call back. We said goodbye, and as I sat back in my recliner, suddenly, I felt the tiniest spark of hope I might be able to survive this.

HERBERT "SHAWN" MILLER

Chapter 8

ON MY WAY to meet Mrs. B., which is how I'll refer to my therapist, I nearly changed my mind and turned around. Although I'd related the details of my attack and the events leading up to it to several people, those had all been friends or family. The thought of telling those same details—some of them embarrassing and demeaning—with a complete stranger and having her ask all kinds of personal, probing questions, kind of freaked me out. I wasn't even sure I believed in psychotherapy…but I needed help learning how to deal with the haunting memories, figuring out a way to regain my perspective, and finding the path back to recapture my former joy. Those thoughts kept me moving forward, determined to keep my appointment.

Mrs. B. and I met at a local Denny's I'd frequented many times in the past. After greeting each other and exchanging pleasantries, we sat down in a booth toward the back, away from the door.

"Why don't we order some food?" she suggested. "I haven't had lunch, and I'm starving. Do you mind talking in between bites?"

She smiled, and I decided then and there I liked this woman. She seemed down to earth and easygoing.

"Sounds good to me."

We motioned for our waitress, placed our order, and then sipped cups of fresh coffee while we waited for our meals.

"I don't mean to insult you," I said, "but I was wondering how you'd feel about signing a non-disclosure agreement. What I'm about to tell you concerns someone very well known, and I wouldn't want any of the details to get out."

Mrs. B. shook her head. "That's totally unnecessary, you know. Therapists are bound by the same HIPAA laws as other doctors. Those privacy laws protect your patient rights, and not only can I not reveal anything about your physical or mental health, including personal details you might share with me, but I have to actively protect that information, too. In addition, I could lose my license to practice if I were to reveal anything you happen to tell me."

I'd heard of HIPAA before, but I hadn't known the law applied to therapists. When I thought about it though, it made sense. Considering some of the extremely personal things patients covered with their therapists, the HIPAA rules were probably important safeguards that allowed patients to speak more freely.

Feeling confident I'd voiced all my concerns and had received adequate answers, I began to speak freely in between bites of my Grand Slamwich breakfast sandwich. Mrs. B. sat silently, slowly devouring a plate of fluffy pancakes, listening as I talked.

As I'd done the previous few times I'd told someone about the events onboard the ship, I provided every detail I could recall and described them fully. What I'd done, what Britto had done, what I'd thought, and what I'd believed he had been thinking…I covered it all. I even told the therapist about what had happened with Katherine and what Britto had said when I'd called him from the ship in Puerto Rico. Mrs. B. only interrupted my monologue a few times in order to ask a question or clarify some detail or another.

When I finished my entire, sordid tale, I glanced at my watch and cringed. An hour and a half had passed since we'd taken our seats in the booth. No doubt about it; this therapy stuff would end up costing me a fortune. But if it worked, I'd pay whatever it cost.

And damn, I felt as if a heavy weight had been lifted off my chest, knowing I'd finally divulged my secret to someone who might be able to do more than just listen and offer their sympathy and emotional support. Maybe I'd finally get some help.

At the end of our meal, Ms. B smiled and reached across the table to put her hand on mine.

"I can't make any guarantees, obviously, but after hearing your story, I believe I can help you. I would like the opportunity to try," she said, holding my gaze.

Unable to speak past the lump in my throat, I nodded my consent. The idea I may be able to get beyond the events of that horrible evening on the Norwegian reignited my hope in my future. I longed for the man I'd been before I'd boarded that ship. A strong, capable man who met life head on and enjoyed every minute of it.

"I think it's best I give you my cellphone number." Mrs. B. dug around in her large black purse that looked more like a backpack and probably served the same function. After rifling through a seemingly endless number of and pouches and pockets, she pulled a white business card from an inside slot and held it out to me. "The second number on the bottom is my personal cell. For a while, at least, I want you to call me any time, day or night, if you feel like you need to talk. That's especially true if you sense you're on the verge of having a panic attack or breakdown…or you're having those thoughts about hurting yourself again." She went into her purse again, pulled out a twenty-dollar bill, and stuck it under the edge of her plate.

"I really appreciate you taking the time to meet with me here," I told her, following her lead and pulling a few fives from my wallet. "To be honest, I had my doubts about seeing a therapist, but now that we've met and I've talked to you… Well, I feel a little better. A little hopeful."

"That's a good start. Hold onto that thought!" She grabbed her purse and slid from the booth. "And in the meantime, I'll have my secretary give you a call tomorrow to set up a time for our next in-person appointment, okay?"

"Perfect." I got to my feet and followed her out into the bright afternoon sunshine, my heart somewhat lighter than it had been in weeks.

***

As it turned out, I phoned Mrs. B. a dozen times over the next several days. I called in the morning, in the afternoon, and several times throughout the night. Having someone there for me when the sun went down was a godsend. During the day, I had other things to do, and other people around me most of the time, and usually, I could find enough distractions to keep me from getting lost in my own head. But my inability to sleep left me alone and feeling as if I were the only one in the entire world still awake, pacing the floor, getting in and out of the shower, or mindlessly scrolling through the television channels. The darkness seemed to bring on my nightmare, and the pain I carried around all the time grew more intense.

I'd come to recognize the symptoms of an impending panic attack—tightness in my chest, a racing heartbeat, hot flashes, and an intense feeling of doom. In those moments, no one could convince me I wasn't about to suffer a deadly stroke or heart attack. No one, that was, until I called Mrs. B.

When she answered, I'd launch right into a tirade. All my self-pity, anger, disgust—with myself and others—and depression would come spilling out. Venting to the therapist never failed to release the tension that had built up inside me, and once I stopped talking, she'd spend several minutes giving me advice, asking me questions, and reminding me that no one, anywhere, had ever died of a panic attack. She had one of those soothing voices that could lull any normal person into a deep sleep, but I was far from normal those days. Still, she managed to calm and reassure me every time. Most importantly, she reminded me of something I often forgot…that I'd done nothing—not one single thing—to deserve Britto's attack.

"No one deserves to be the victim of a sexual assault," she'd tell me. "The idea that a woman dressed too provocatively or a man had accepted an invitation to another man's room and therefore, they deserved what they got, is an absolute lie. The courts don't accept those kinds of bullshit excuses, so you shouldn't, either."

Soon, touching base—or talking for hours—to Mrs. B. became both a necessity for me and one of my highest monthly expenses, second only to my mortgage. She charged an hourly rate, and considering how often I called her and how long I talked sometimes, I imagined I was her highest-paying client. Eventually, she and I discussed the problem, and since we both agreed I needed to continue my therapy, Ms. B. agreed to set a monthly rate for me. Thank God. If she hadn't made it more affordable for me to continue working with her as often as I needed to, who knows what might have happened over the following months.

***

The following summer, I almost made a life-altering, life-ending decision.

Roughly six months had passed since our last cruise, and in all that time, I'd barely gotten any sleep and rarely could describe myself as feeling relaxed and at ease. My mind was always preoccupied with what had happened that night aboard the ship. Like a broken record, the images would scroll through my mind over and over, and I'd analyze each action—both his and mine—and try to come up with a reason. Why had he chosen me? What had I done to attract his unwanted attention? What could I have done or said differently?

My heart ached, but the rest of me felt numb. I continued spending hours a day in the shower, my sanctuary and the only place I felt truly clean. The only place that disgusting, dirty odor couldn't invade my senses. And if I wasn't in the shower, I would spend hours just lying in bed and reliving those hours that had completely changed my life. Where do I go from here? How do I heal myself and stop this pain? Unwanted and unbidden, thoughts of suicide continued to plague me, like some sinister voice whispering in my ear, "End your life and you'll end the pain."

One morning, I came close to acting on that advice. I was working out, and since I was doing legs, I had my ankles weights on. Without warning, that dirty, musky odor assailed me, so strong I glanced around, fearing I would see Britto standing somewhere close by. Although I was alone and not in danger, something within me snapped. I leaned down, took the heaviest set of dumbbells I owned, and attached one to each of the ankle-weight straps.

Water. I need to get in the water. That'll wash away the smell. Water...

Instead of heading down the hall toward the shower, I went outside onto the patio that surrounded our inground swimming pool. I had to drag my feet, and the weights along with them, as they were too heavy for me to lift each time I needed to take a step.

A soft breeze rippled the surface of the pool, and the bright sunlight made the water shimmer and sparkle like it was covered in diamonds. Mesmerized by the beauty, I stepped to the edge.

Go ahead, that sinister voice whispered. *Jump in. All those memories will disappear, and so will your pain.*

I jumped.

The moment my body sliced through the tepid water, I sank straight to the bottom, the weights around my ankles drawing me downward. I'd chosen to jump into the deepest end, and water covered my head. For a moment, I held my breath and tried to calm the terror that caused my heart to race. *It's okay. A few minutes of discomfort, and it'll all be over.*

But my will to live overruled my decision to end it all. I began thrashing and trying to kick, using my arms to compensate for my weighted-down legs to try to make it back to the surface. *God, I'm so sorry! Please help me get out of here. I don't want to die!*

All my floundering around did nothing but cause my chest to tighten and my lungs to ache. *The weights, you idiot! Take off the ankle weights.*

The pain in my chest grew worse, and my lungs burned. I fought the instinct to open my mouth and inhale. *Wait. Wait. Wait. Wait. Wait.* I leaned down and managed to release the straps around one of my ankles, and the weight fell free. But I had run out of time. I needed air. Now.

I turned my head, frantic to find a way up and out. Behind me, not five feet away, was the blue-painted cement wall of the pool. I drew on every last bit of strength and struggled over to the side. As darkness started to cloud my vision, I reached up and grasped the edge with my fingertips. I pulled with all my might and dragged myself up and over the ledge, and I flopped face forward onto the rough concrete. I rolled onto my back, gasping for air. I took a couple long, deep breaths and closed my eyes against the sun's glare. Tears slipped from beneath my closed lids and trickled down my face.

How stupid... Why had I tried to do something that would have destroyed my family's entire world? Thank God, I'd managed to get out, and no one was home to witness one of the darkest, weakest moments of my life. I didn't really want to die. I wanted to live long enough to see my daughters marry and to hold my grandchildren. But that voice inside me, the one that sounded like a demon and urged me to end my life, had taken a firm hold. I had to learn how to recognize when I wasn't in control, when I was losing the battle. To help calm my still racing heart, I brought forth the image of my daughters' faces. Their bright smiles warmed me inside. Those girls were worth living forth. I had to continue the fight. But how could I when the pain hadn't lessened, and I still couldn't sleep, despite the passage of time? How much longer could I go on like this? I still carried around so much anger...with Britto and with myself. Why the hell hadn't I reacted more strongly to his advances? Why hadn't I kicked his ass? Knocked him out? Thrown him over the damn railing and into the ocean? Would that have made things better? Would my life be easier now, or would I be locked up in a prison somewhere, awaiting a trial for murder or manslaughter?

I drew in a deep breath and screamed, releasing my frustrations in one long, loud, heartbroken cry.

Oddly enough, I felt better after that, and a little calmer. *Count your blessings.* So many of my friends and family members would probably remind me I had so much to live for, and no matter how bad things might seem, they could always be worse.

I started listing all the good things in my world and sending up prayers of thanks. God had allowed me to find my way out of the swimming pool. He had saved me from my own stupidity, and He'd taken away some of the pain... He'd given me a kind and faithful wife and three beautiful daughters. And He had given me things to look forward to in the future if I had the guts to stick around long enough. One day, I would walk each of my girls down the aisle and watch them get married. I would be there for the births of all my grandchildren...

Exhausted from so much emotional turmoil, I kept my eyes closed and imagined those future babies with their chubby cheeks and impossibly tiny toes. That made me smile. Would I prefer they called me Grandpa, Granddad, or Grandfather? Maybe Papa? I didn't really care, as long as they spoke to me with love.

At some point, I must have drifted off. The sound of my dogs barking made me jerk, and my eyes flew open. Where am I? I looked around, momentarily confused, and then I recalled what I'd done. Shame filled me with the desire to hide all the evidence before my wife or the girls got home.

I scrambled to my feet and quickly removed weights from my other leg. The ones I'd removed in the water were still there, lying on the bottom of the pool. I leaped in, dove down, and retrieved them, and then I climbed back out and took everything back into the house.

Even after managing to get a little sleep, I was still a little out of it, so I headed for my room and jumped into the shower—the only place I still felt safe and calm.

***

I'd heard the term PTSD before, but Ms. B explained what it meant when she diagnosed me with this disorder during one of our sessions.

Saying I have PTSD doesn't fully describe what I go through. I suffer from this ailment daily, and after a while, even those constant calls to my therapist began to exacerbate my symptoms. Every time I relived those events, either in my head or through conversation, was a form of torture. I had fallen into a nearly constant cycle of talking, thinking, or journaling about what Britto had done to me, trying to find an outlet for the emotions that resurfaced either on their own or following a counseling session. Even with therapy, I began to feel as if I lived inside my head. After one of my counseling sessions with Ms. B., I didn't even make it out of the parking lot before once again, I found myself trapped inside my mind. I relived those horrendous events again, and as I sat in my Jeep Rubicon, I kept asking myself the same question. Why? How could I have allowed that man to hold me hostage inside his cabin, and why had he done such a thing? What world did Romero Britto live in? Certainly not the same one I inhabited. Apparently, Britto occupied a space where the rich and famous can do whatever they wish and suffer very little or no repercussions. In the world I live in, no means no. Stop means stop. During the session I'd had with Ms. B right before I broke down in my car, I did find some clarity and certainty regarding what went on that fateful night. Together, she and I had listened to the recording I had made on my cellphone, and what I heard validated what I'd always believed. What happened night was not my fault, and I was not to blame for any of it. Ms. B. and I did a tally, and I had said "no" fifty-eight times, and I'd said stop, quit, and other words to that effect twenty-eight times. Repeatedly, I told him I would not consent to his advances, and I had never urged him to touch me or given him permission to do so. Despite my protestation, he'd continued to try to coerce me into having sex with him.

How would the world and all the admirers of his work see him if they knew what he'd done? I sat in my car and thought about the idea of telling more people. If I were a woman, would I feel more empowered to speak? As a Black if I came forward, could I make a difference in other men's lives? Or would I be ostracized, criticized, and called a liar? All these questions depressed me, taking me down into a pit of despair hard and fast. Sick and tired of feeling helpless and useless, I pulled myself together and drove out of the parking lot. I only made it a mile or so before I broke down again. I've discovered I'm often triggered when I'm driving, which forces me to pull off onto the side of the road as quickly as possible. As if my entire world comes to a halt, I lose control of myself. Thanks to intense therapy, I've learned to recognize some of my personal triggers. I've also discovered a likely reason why they put me in such an out-of-control emotional state and then immediately force me back to that night. Normally, after one of these breakdowns, or episodes or whatever some people might call them, I become very upset with myself. I'll stand in front of the bathroom mirror and stare in disgust at my reflection, or I'll sit frozen in my car and yell at myself, which usually involves questioning my strength, courage, and worth as a man.

"Why are you letting that fucker control your life? You are a weak motherfucker! Quit being such a pussy, you little baby."

During a recent session, my therapist asked me what I did when I found myself in such a hopeless emotional state or in the middle of a full-blown breakdown.

I ducked my head and couldn't look her in the eyes. She wouldn't be pleased when I told her. "I gamble," I mumbled.

Ms. B. didn't say anything, but I could sense her disapproval. Thankfully, we'd formed a bond of trust by that point, so I went on, describing how I'd discovered gambling helped ward off the memories and the panic attacks, and the emotional breakdowns.

"I bet and play hand after hand until my negative feelings disappear." I shrugged.

"And what emotions does gambling make you feel instead?

"Sometimes, I feel happier, and sometimes, I'm just numb enough to keep going."

However, developing a gambling addiction as a way to cope with PTSD symptoms wasn't the smartest idea I'd come up with, and it couldn't go on indefinitely.

For one thing, all that wasted money hurt the people closest to me the most. But at the time, I was desperate, and it was the only thing I found that helped to curb my PTSD symptoms. I played hands I should have folded, but for me, playing poker was never about winning. I sat at the tables night after night to experience the rush of adrenaline. Like a uptick in serotonin, it felt a lot better than facing the thoughts that were awaiting me when I stopped finding distractions to fill every waking moment.

At some point, many weeks into my gambling addiction, I looked through my recent old bank statements, credit card bills, and savings withdrawals to try to get a handle on how much I'd lost. The total, nearly six figures, made me sick to my stomach and even more depressed. I needed to stop, but if I did that, I'd be right back to where I was, facing all my demons nearly twenty-four hours a day. As I write this, I am actively working to overcome my gambling addiction. Dealing with the depression was one of the most difficult things I have ever tried to do.

When I thought about what an acute problem I'd developed, I had a brief conversation with my brother, who happens to be a drug addict.

"I think I'd rather have your addiction than mine,' I told him.

"Why's that?" He looked at me as if I was crazy.

"Because it's a hell of a lot cheaper," I said, but even to me, that sounded like a copout. Rather than dwelling on the cost of an individual addiction—because it really didn't matter—I should be getting to the root of the problems that had caused me to start gambling in the first place. Only by facing those and figuring out a way to put them behind me, would I ever be able to move on.

During my counseling sessions with Ms. B we covered many topics but everything always led back to the trauma brought on by Romero Britto. At 51 years of age, I look and feel better than I have in years. I attempt to workout at least three times a week, and I eat pretty healthy foods. But my current life is a reflection of what Britto did to me months ago, and I needed to figure out what it will take so I can move on.

The vacation aboard the Norwegian should have been one of the best events in my life, and instead, those days and nights spent on the ocean resulted in a nightmare that continued to haunt me months and then years later.

I'd been one of those people who believed that sexual assault doesn't happen to someone who looks like me. I'd been blindsided that night, and I hadn't seen what was coming for many reasons. For one thing, I'm a fighter. I loved pitting my strength and skills against an opponent, and I'm proud about the fact I've always done pretty well. Most of the time when I'm out somewhere, other guys don't mess with me. They see I'm a pretty big man…strong…and they don't start any shit. Yet, when Britto assaulted me, I forgot every self-defense tactic I'd ever mastered. My self-preservation instincts had completely disappeared. Secondly, somehow, I'd missed Britto's true intentions when he'd befriended me. His fame and status had given me confidence I could trust him and wold be safe around him.

One question haunts me… Had Britto targeted me that night because I was Black? Statistically, Black men don't come forward in these situations. Pride, a history of being subjected to pedophiles—and having those experiences swept under the rug, and deep-rooted homophobia that permeates the Black community keep a lot of men from speaking out. After my assault, I surrounded myself with a protective shield made of fear. I was afraid I'd be ostracized by my friends and my community, afraid people would assume I was gay, or I'd be persecuted for daring to accuse such a famous artist of such a malicious act.

I thought back to my own projections and the opinions I had in the past. Would people blame me when they discovered my attack had occurred in the middle of the night? As a society, we haven't fully gotten past our old prejudices, one of which states that a man or woman who agrees to go to the home or room of someone of the opposite sex at that late hour could have only wanted one thing. I'm ashamed to admit, I'd had those same thoughts. Right up to the point I'd become a victim.

At this point in my story, I'd like to make a formal apology to Desiree Washington. I was a young man when her story surfaced, and I agreed with a large portion of the world's population that she knew what she was getting into when she put herself in that room with Mike Tyson in the middle of the night. I didn't believe her when she called it rape. So, Ms. Washington, I am deeply sorry. After experiencing something similar, I would stand beside you and all the other men and women who've been victimized and assaulted. It shouldn't have taken that much for me to develop a greater understanding. But I can see clearer now that I am a part of the Me Too Movement…now that I've become a part of the Ninety-Three Percent. Truly, I wish I had stood up sooner.

Chapter 9

WHY ME?

FEAR OF COMING forward to share my story isn't the only thing that keeps me at a standstill. I'm also afraid I won't ever be able to *move* forward. PTSD has taken control of my life and controls all my actions. I have always been known as the happy, fun-loving friend, full of laughter and always ready to brighten someone's day with a good joke. So much has changed since December 10, 2019. Now, I am completely consumed by sadness. I spend hours in a lost in a dark place, and even when I'm smiling, I find it hard to breathe, as if a horse is stepping on my chest. My vision is narrow, and I can't see where the darkness ends and the light begins. One person took away my ability to control my own destiny. He took away so damn much, and I feel so helpless.

While I am trying to cope with my new diagnoses of depression and PTSD, Romero Britto's life continues, unshattered. While I spend hours in the driver's seat of my car, sobbing into the silence, Romero Britto laughs his way through an interview. While I still spend hours upon hours in the shower, trying to wash his filth off me, Romero Britto shares online forums with former political figure, Jeb Bush. While I use my money to pay for extensive therapy, Britto continues to paint and earn money from the sales of those works and even finds time to update his Facebook status. He is completely unbothered, while I've spent the last few years searching for some sort of normalcy again.

***

One day, during a therapy session, Ms. B. and I were sitting in a couple of comfortable chairs in her office when she brought up the subject of closure.

"Closure doesn't mean the exact same thing for everyone," she said. "Some people need to confront their attacker, while others are satisfied with writing a detailed letter they never intend to mail, and still others want to seek justice through legal channels."

I nodded. "That makes sense. There are probably as many different variations as there are victims."

"Right. So, what do you think? Are you willing to try to find some closure, and if you are, what does that look like for you?"

"I'd love to put this behind me," I said. "And I've been thinking about this pretty much since the day Romero—"

"No." Ms. B. interrupted me and shook her head. "Not Romero Britto. Not yet anyway. For you to really put the past behind you and find a way to deal with your trauma, you'll have to go all the way back to when you were nine years old. That experience played a large role in both how you dealt with what happened to you when Britto held you, hostage, in his room, and the way your mind has processed those events since then. Before you can deal with him, you'll have to find closure with the neighbor who molested you and inflicted so much emotional and psychological damage."

"You're right. I know you're right, but there's just one problem. David, my child molester ex-neighbor, went to prison a long time ago. I don't think he's still alive." I sighed then added, "Isn't that just my luck? I need closure with him before I can deal with my current situation, but I'll never be able to do that because the guy dropped dead."

"That's one way of looking at it," Ms. B. said. "But you could also think about it this way… David received the ultimate punishment. Maybe not for his crimes against you, but he *was* punished. And if he died in prison, well, that's all the more reason to believe he paid a high price for his crimes." She paused then added, "But remember what we both said earlier—closure can mean something different to every victim. So what do you think, Shawn? If your neighbor died in prison while serving time for some other crime he committed, does that allow you to move past what he did to you when you were a boy?"

I thought about what she said for a few minutes, and she sat and waited for me. That was another thing I appreciated about her—she had more patience than anyone I'd ever known. If I needed time to come to terms with some new piece of information or to carefully consider an answer to a question—like now for example—she never rushed me. If I were still paying her by the hour, that would make sense, but even after she switched me to a flat monthly fee, she never said or did anything to make me feel rushed.

After a couple of minutes, I nodded slowly. "When you put it that way, I suppose it does. I mean, a tiny part of me wishes I could have tracked him down and confronted him, but so much time has passed, and I doubt he remembers me as well as I recall him and the things he made me do." I paused and shivered in disgust. "But mainly, I want to come to terms with what happened, fill in all the blanks, which you and I can do during our sessions I hope, and then I'd like to bury it again, put it all back in that box my mind obviously created when I was a kid so I'd have half a chance to grow up somewhat normal. Unlike what happened on the ship, I'd never blame myself for what happened back then. I was a boy, and David was a grown man. He earned my trust, and then he manipulated, coerced, and sometimes forced me to take part in doing unspeakable things. I had no choice but to go along with what he wanted. I mean, it's not as if I could have fought back or told someone. Who would take the word of a little kid over that of an adult with the reputation of a fine, helpful, upstanding part of the neighborhood?" I nodded again, more forcefully this time. "Yes, I can put a period at the end of this and move on. I don't have any unanswered questions or think there are any loose ends that need to be tied up."

Ms. B. smiled and patted my knee. "That's wonderful! I'm really happy to hear you say those things. Don't be upset or surprised if memories of those encounters come to mind now and then. All you need to do is remind yourself of everything you just told me, and you'll be fine." She glanced at the notepad she had balanced on her knees and then looked up at me and smiled. "So...what do you think? Are you ready to move on? I'll ask the same questions in regard to Britto. What could he say or do, or what would you like to see happen that would provide you with a bit of closure in that instance?"

I'd thought about this question many times since that night on the ship, so she didn't have to wait for me to think this one over. I had an answer ready for her.

"All I've ever wanted..." I paused as a lump formed in my throat, and my eyes started stinging. God, why was this so much more difficult than dealing with David's abuse? Maybe because even now, although I recognized the truth and had remembered many vivid details, I could still imagine, if only for a few minutes, that those things had happened to someone else. Each time another memory resurfaced, I reviewed the details and tried to place the events into the timeline of my childhood. Sometimes I could, and sometimes I couldn't, but in every case, I felt distanced from those years of my life and much more capable of coping with what my brain saw fit to reveal.

I glanced over at Ms. B. and cleared my throat. "Sorry... As I was saying, the only thing I've wanted was for him to listen and really hear me, to accept the blame, and to validate my feelings instead of trying to say I was imagining things or blowing things out of proportion, and for him to offer a genuine apology for his behavior."

"That makes a lot of sense. To add insult to injury, he denied he knew you then claimed he'd been drunk and couldn't recall what had happened. If he'd take responsibility, that would probably ease some of the pain you're carrying around like a necklace made of lead." She leaned forward in her chair and grabbed my hand. "What do you think? Should we give him a call?"

"We?" I asked, not understanding her question.

She laughed. "Well, you'll make the call, but I'll be here for moral support. Well, can you So...do you think you can handle it?"

"Yes. I guess I am, and I think I can. I mean, I'm more than ready to find some closure, but honestly, I'm a little afraid to make the phone call." I paused and looked down, ashamed at how pathetic and weak I sounded. But I had several concerns. Like, how would I react when I heard his voice again? Or what if the conversation went south, and he threatened me? "Well," I said, addressing myself as well as my therapist, "I guess the only way I'll ever know is to call him.

I pulled my cell phone out of the pocket of my sweatshirt and scrolled through my contacts until I reached Britto's name. My hands started shaking a little, but I pushed through my fear. I tapped on his name then on the tiny, old-fashioned phone handset icon in the upper area of the screen. I took a deep breath to calm my rattled nerves then put my phone to my ear.

WHY ME?

The phone rang three times. *It's going to go to voicemail,* I thought, and a part of me would've been just fine with that. On the other hand, if I didn't get to talk to him, I'd never get any closure.

I started to pull the phone away from my ear so I could end the call when he answered.

"Hi, Shawn."

Obviously, he'd programmed my name and number into his phone, too.

"Hello," I said, but then my mind went blank. What should I say to the monster who'd tried to rape me and then denied remembering a single detail of those events? Before I could come up with something that would sound good, Britto started talking.

"I really want to apologize. I mean, I need to say I'm sorry. I never meant to hurt you, and I believe we can be good friends. I really am sorry for my actions, and I am asking for your forgiveness." He sucked in a harsh breath and went on before I could say a word. "Shawn, you must know I would never hurt you, that I'd never try to harm you in any way."

His words were like a soothing ointment applied to the wounds he'd inflicted on my mind, heart, and soul. Almost immediately, I felt more alive, invigorated, and confident. All this time, I'd been walking around feeling like he'd placed shackles around my ankles and my wrists, and now, finally, he'd handed me the key to free myself from the hold he'd had on me.

As Britto continued telling me how bad he'd felt and how sorry he was, I glanced over at Ms. B. and raised my eyebrows, signaling my surprise. She grinned and gave me a thumbs up then mouthed the words, "You're doing great!" I nodded, and tears of joy rolled down my cheeks. Finally! Britto had finally admitted he'd been wrong, and he was actually asking for my forgiveness. Up until that moment, I hadn't believed I'd ever hear him utter those words. But I needed a little more from him before I could really call this closure.

"Romero?" I said, "I'd like to tell you how I felt that night. Would you listen while I speak?"

I held my breath and waited for him to respond.

"Yes, yes! Of course. Whatever you need and whatever I can do to make it up to you."

For the next several minutes, he didn't say a word, as I described how I'd felt when I realized he had a different motive for inviting me to his room that evening. I described the sense of outrage and betrayal that had filled me, and then I told him how I'd felt demeaned, dirty, and disgusted when he'd made one sexual advance after another, despite the fact I had repeatedly told him I wasn't interested. When I finished talking, the heavy burden I'd carried with me for so long seemed a lot lighter. Like a feather compared to a load of bricks… But it was time to wrap this up.

"Well, Romero, I really appreciate you taking my call, and I'm grateful you gave me the opportunity to express my feelings about what went on that night. I accept your apology," I told him. "I've got to get going. I was in the middle of an appointment when I—"

Britto interrupting my attempt to get off the phone said "Always willing to listen to a friend", "**But Shawn, you know we're both adults and what occurred between us was consensual.**" My thought goes immediately to *Did you just say that?*

With those few words, he turned my world upside down again. I'd have to continue dealing with all the horrible thoughts and feelings I'd been suffering from since that awful night. He had apologized, but then in just seconds he negated every word he'd said about being sorry for what he'd done.

Fresh tears streamed down my face, but joy was no longer the driving emotion. My chest hurt, and I put a hand above my heart and massaged the pain.

"You son-of-a-bitch!" I erupted in rage. "How fucking *dare* you? That apology didn't mean shit, did it? That was just another one of your attempts to manipulate me. Fifty-eight times, you lame excuse for a human being—I asked you to stop fifty-fucking-eight times, and you refused to listen. Do you call that shit consensual? How about the twenty-nine times I asked you to let me go and to quit stopping me from leaving? Was that consensual, also?"

Across from me, Ms. B. started waving her hands back and forth, and then ran a finger across her neck, which I took to indicate she wanted me to end the call. When I didn't comply right away, she gently peeled the phone out of my grip and pressed the button to disconnect.

I crumpled like a wet paper towel. Leaning forward, I covered my face with my hands and rocked back and forth.

The sobs filled my chest before bursting forth in a long, plaintive wail, the kind of sound that comes from the depths of a person's soul when they learn about the death of a loved one.

Ms. B. put both hands on my shoulders and gently lifted me until we sat face to face. I sucked in a couple of shaky breaths and tried to regain my composure.

"You will be okay," she told me. "You're strong, and we'll find another way to help you get past this."

I forced a tremulous smile and wiped my wet cheeks with my hands. "I'll be okay. He shocked me, that's all. And my gut tells me the only reason he took my call or apologized was because he found an attorney who gave that piece of shit advice on how to handle this."

"You're probably right. So, what now? Do you have any idea how you'd like to proceed?"

"Yes…believe it or not, I do. Before you brought up the idea of trying to get closure by contacting Britto, I'd been thinking of ways to vindicate myself. I wondered if other people knew what happened, would they believe me, or would I become a different kind of victim all over again? I ended up deciding it didn't matter." I caught and held her gaze. "I want to tell my story to the world. I want to reveal what he did to me because it might prevent someone else from becoming that deviant's next victim. And if other people read the book and they believe me, all the better."

"You're going to write a book?" Ms. B. raised a brow. "That's quite an undertaking. But if it helps you find closure, I think you should do it."

I nodded as I began running ideas through my head. I still couldn't believe that asshole had tried to blame the events of that night on both of us. Two consenting adults, my ass. His attempt to frame things in that light verified aspects of his personality I'd already suspected. He felt entitled as if he could do anything he wanted to do and suffer no repercussions. Had he been born with those narcissistic tendencies, or had he developed that attitude once he'd achieved money and fame? Probably a combination of both…

The tightness in my chest had started to ease, thankfully. This shit would end up causing me to have a heart attack if I didn't find a way to cope. Others who have gone through something similar probably know exactly how I feel. An apology followed by untruthful justification wasn't any kind of apology at all. And if Britto couldn't give me what I needed to come to terms with what he'd done to me if I couldn't make him hear me and understand, then I'd tell my story and the world would hear me. In the end, I hoped to rediscover my sanity.

***

That night, I started writing. At first, I told myself I was writing it all down to work through the pain with no thoughts toward publication. But then I learned about a man by the name of Terry Crews and about the support he received from the Me Too Movement after he'd come forward as a victim of sexual assault.

Terry Crews was an actor and former NFL player, and I ran across an article he'd written in 2016.

The more I learned about Terry Crews, the more I related to his story, and my desire to come forward with my truth intensified. Not only had he been a victim of sexual assault, but like me, he was a strong Black man. As someone who'd become a household name, he'd felt a lot of pressure to keep quiet about his experience, but he hadn't listened. His decision to share his story inspired me and cemented my decision to take a stand, publicly reveal what had happened to me, and hold my attacker accountable.

The first step I took toward taking a stand and speaking out happened on December 19, 2020, at exactly 5:00 a.m. The timing is incredibly significant to me because exactly twenty-four hours prior, I had lost my mother. She had been ill for weeks before her passing and had missed Thanksgiving with the family due to an extended hospital stay. Right around the time Mom got sick, my wife had booked a room for me in a Miami hotel located a few miles away from Romero Britto's art studio. Although my wife was not going to be able to be a part of the protests I'd put together—she had planned a trip away with one of her best friends, and I urged her to keep her commitment—she was still very proud of my effort to take charge of my life and find a way to move forward. I had rallied the support of some of my personal friends, all of whom would be there. Those friends reached out to other people they knew, and we put together a group made up of a decent number of individuals who join me for the drive down to Miami, rally behind me, and help me make sure my voice and story were heard.

On Friday, December 18, my wife left for the airport before sunrise. I walked her to our front door and kissed her goodbye, and then I went back to sleep. A few hours later, I woke up and checked my phone for the time, but something else caught my attention. According to the lock screen on my cell, I had slept through at least twenty missed calls from my sisters, and just recently, right at five o'clock, I'd missed three calls in a row from my wife. While the phone was still in my hand, she called again.

"Hello! Kelly? Are you okay?" I held my cell in a tight grip.

"I-I I'm fine," she answered in a broken voice. "But I'm afraid I've got some bad news. Your mom just passed away."

Even though Mom had been sick, the news still came as a shock. I sat in silence for several seconds, trying to process what I'd just heard.

"I'll catch the next available flight back," Kelly told me. "And I'm guessing you won't feel like driving down to Miami tomorrow morning…"

"No! You stay where you are, at least for now, and try to have a good time. At least relax. I'm going down to Miami and see this thing through." In my heart, the protest I'd planned needed to happen, maybe now more than ever. I could sense my mother's spirit urging me to go, and if she were there right then, she would have said the same thing.

So the very next day, on December 19, exactly twenty-four hours after my mother's passing, my friends and family and I loaded up in a few SUVs and made the five-hour drive down to Miami. We had posted on social media about the silent protest we were holding and had encouraged others in the Miami area to join us.

During that long drive, we all grew a little anxious about how the people near Britto's studio would receive us. Again, I wondered if others would believe my story. Would people rally behind me after they discovered the name of the person I was accusing? Especially once they saw me and got a look at my muscular physique and the color of my skin. With these disturbing questions bombarding my mind, I kept quiet for most of the ride and played music on the stereo to help distract me and ease some of my tension.

Before we knew it, we had arrived at the hotel, and the strangest thing happened. The uncertainty that had dogged me throughout the trip disappeared entirely. For lack of a better description, suddenly, I felt pumped. The minute my feet hit the ground in Miami, I was ready to take a stand. Our hotel was only a few minutes away from Britto's studio, so we dropped our luggage off in our rooms, got right back into the cars, and drove directly to the address where Britto rented a storefront. As we neared the area where we planned to hold our two-day protest, I knew we'd made a good choice in deciding to use silence to attract attention. Britto's studio was in the heart of Miami's commercial area, surrounded by other shopping venues, restaurants, and outdoor eateries. His building faced a fountain and a small patch of grass adorned with statues and various seating areas. The park-like setting attracted groups of people of all ages and seemed generally quiet. We weren't there to make a scene and had no intention of disturbing the peace. Instead, we were there to shine a light of truth on the bright, colorful world Britto had created for himself, behind which he hid things that were dark and ugly. I believed we'd make a strong statement by holding our signs and standing silently beside his place of business. We didn't have to scream or yell or even say a word; the signs we'd created screamed the truth about Britto to anyone who bothered to stop and read.

We lined up with me in the center and my friends and family spaced out on either side. As people from all walks of life passed by us and read the picket-style signs we held, we smiled and nodded but kept silent. Each sign reflected something I'd either said to Britto that night or had tried to convey to him since then.

STOP MEANS STOP!

FALSE IMPRISONMENT IS A CRIME!

IF SOMEONE SAYS "NO" 58 TIMES WHILE BEING HELD AGAINST THEIR WILL, THAT MEANS IT WAS NOT CONSENSUAL

Eventually, our small protest began to attract some attention. For the most part, we remained silent, but when people started to ask what we were doing, I began to speak up. I told the truth, but so as not to incriminate myself, I explained to those who asked what we were protesting that the man who created the paintings filling the studio behind us had sexually assaulted someone. We'd come there to let the public know what he'd done and to be a voice for the victim. I explained that we were taking a stand to let Romero Britto and men like him know they can't sexually assault someone without being held accountable.

Most people supported our cause, which lifted my spirits and gave me hope for my future. But some people were confused, vindictive, or just plain ugly.

One couple walked by on the opposite side of the street, and the man yelled, "Antifa scum!"

At the time of our demonstration, tensions grew when the public caught sight of a group of protestors. Members of the group, Black Lives Matter took over the streets in towns and cities across the country. News stations, ever worried about pleasing their audiences and upping their ratings, constantly played footage of riots and the devastation that was caused in several of these communities. Many members of the public saw only the fires and property damage, thanks to all that media coverage, and they refused to look deeper and examine the root causes. As a result, BLM members continued to hold demonstrations in their fight for fundamental human rights for people of color.

When passersby saw us standing together, some of them yelled racial slurs at my family and I.

Without even reading our signs, one man stood right up in my face and shouted, "All lives matter, you fucking idiot!"

I didn't respond, and neither did any of the others in my group and after a minute, the guy moved on. Apparently, he was satisfied he'd made his point. Of course, we disagreed with him, but that was not our fight at that particular moment.

The later it got, the more people filled the sidewalks. They came to shop or get something to eat at one of several restaurants nearby. But more people meant more yelling and cursing from those who either misunderstood why we were there or who just didn't care enough to read our signs or ask.

Although we maintained our silence, the shouts from others started to attract a small crowd. Eventually, one of Britto's store managers asked us to leave.

"I'm sorry, ma'am," I calmly explained, "but we can't do that. As U.S. citizens, we have a right to demonstrate peacefully."

Clearly unhappy with my response, the woman scowled and stomped off, back inside the store. As the door closed behind her, something told me this wasn't over.

Sure enough, about five minutes later, a man came out of the art studio and made the same request for us to leave. Once again, I politely refused, but instead of going back into the building, the man took out his cell phone and began recording us.

"Why are you doing that?" I asked him. "It's not like we're out here raising hell and damaging property."

The guy didn't answer, so I shrugged and turned my back on him. Let him document our actions. After all, we were both on a public sidewalk, so he had every right to film. And besides, if anyone did call in a complaint, we could use the recording to show we hadn't done anything wrong.

The manager was still recording an hour later—this time from behind the cover of a nearby tree trunk—when another man, who also said he was a manager, rode up on a bicycle. Without dismounting, he started peppering us with questions about why we were there, who we thought we were to stand there with those signs, and make those accusations when we weren't even members of the community. We ignored him, and I hoped he'd give up and go away, but instead, he got off his bike and approached me, his cell phone in hand.

I have to say, the next five minutes or so was a difficult and true test of my commitment to remain silent and peaceful. Holding his phone right up in my face to document my reactions, he made one inciting statement after another. His motive was obvious, at least, to me. He wanted me to say or do something—anything—he could use to show I'd gotten violent, but I wouldn't rise to the bait, and neither would any of my family or friends. If we did, our message would get lost in the chaos that followed, and we'd have wasted all our time and energy.

A few minutes later, five police cars pulled up, and although I was happy to see them, I had to roll my eyes. Ten or more cops to shut down a ten-man silent protest… Talk about excessive use of force!

Several officers left their vehicles and stood nearby to watch for a while, but they never approached us. Were they trying to act intimidating? Maybe hoping their mere presence would cause us to leave? I considered my options, and after a moment, I propped my sign against a nearby post and walked over to the officers to say hello. I figured that would be better than all of us standing on opposite sides of the street, staring at each other like a bunch of kids on the playground.

I approached the closest officer. "Hi. My name's Shawn." I nodded hello, first to him and then to his fellow cops. "I thought I should come over and explain why we're out here holding a silent protest."

"That's a good idea," the police officer next to the one I'd addressed answered. He sounded irritated. "We've received a half dozen complaints about people screaming and causing a scene out here."

I shook my head. "Wasn't us. In fact, we chose to hold a silent protest for exactly that reason. As you can see by the statements on the signs we're holding, we came here to give a message, not to cause any trouble. Despite being screamed at, cursed at, and videotaped, we've all remained completely calm. I did answer questions for a few people, but I never raised my voice."

Out of the corner of my eye, I noticed another officer approaching me. Tall and muscular, he had a commanding presence, and his expression seemed like a mix between amusement and annoyance. When he reached my side, instead of talking to me right away, he addressed the two men I'd been explaining myself to.

"Is this the large group of protesters who are out here causing all kinds of trouble?" he asked, nodding toward where my family and friends still stood on the sidewalk holding their signs.

"Looks like it, sir," the patrolman answered. He looked at me and added, "We were just taking this man's statement."

"Great, that's great," the senior officer said before his subordinate could provide any details. "I'll wait to read all about it when you file your report. Meanwhile, you all clear out of here. I'm certain we've got important calls to handle, and obviously, this isn't one of them."

"But sir—!" the policeman who'd copped an attitude with me tried to get in on the conversation.

The senior officer glared in the man's direction. "'But sir' nothing! I have two eyes, and I can see just fine, and there's no reason for us to be out here right now. Those people aren't causing any trouble, they aren't harassing anybody, and they aren't committing any crimes. Now, clear out!"

I hesitated, but I needed to tell this officer about our plans. "Excuse me, sir? May I have a minute of your time?"

He glanced in my direction then said something to the angry cop that I couldn't make out because he spoke too low for me to hear, and then he came to stand next to me.

"One minute," he said in a gravelly voice, "that's all you get. I've wasted enough time out here already."

"Yes, sir, I understand," I said. "I just wanted to let you know we plan on coming back here again tomorrow. Hopefully, you won't get called out because of us again. I'm really sorry that happened."

The officer's demeanor changed, and he turned his head to look me in the eye. "Not your fault. I know how some people can be… always looking for trouble, and if they can't find any, they start some themselves. What are you protesting?"

Surprised he asked, I ended up telling him the same half-truth I'd told the pedestrians earlier. When I finished, he nodded and pulled a business card out of his shirt pocket.

"Here. That's my direct number on the back. Give me a call before you head out in the morning, and I'll send a patrol officer down to keep an eye on things and make sure your people are safe and no one gets hurt."

Once again, he'd knocked me off my stride, this time with his unexpected offer. I would have never expected kindness or support from a man who looked like a cross between Mr. Clean and a large bull. Stocky, bald, and built like a tank, he looked like a stereotypical, redneck, Deep South cop. The kind of guy who'd sooner kick my ass and throw me in cuffs than offer to provide me with security. Then again, I should have known better. I'd learned a long time ago, things aren't always how they appear.

"Thank you." I tucked the card into my back-pants pocket and smiled. "Nice seeing you, Officer."

"Sergeant!" he said correcting me as of his rank in that deep, rough voice.

"Yes, sir, Sergeant, sir." I turned and hustled back over to grab my sign and continue with our protest.

For the remainder of that day, I couldn't stop smiling. The commanding officer's response to our presence and to me, directly, made me certain we were doing the right thing, and despite the noise made by angry people who were simply looking for a reason to complain, we were reaching a lot of others who got our message and offered supportive comments.

***

Throughout the second day of our protest, several people stopped to talk to us and to share personal stories about their encounters with Britto, and most described him as a rude and pompous man. Other people paused to read the signs we held and then told us the accusations we were making didn't surprise them because they had heard rumors. Shocked by these statements, I had to wonder how many victims Britto had left behind him as he traveled the world, flaunting his power and money. A firm belief formed in my mind; *I was not his first.*

An older woman in a long, flowing, purple wrap-around cover-up stopped to say how sorry she was for the victim of our story.

"I've heard similar things about that man for as long as I can remember," she added.

Her statement immediately took me back to a phone call I'd had with Mr. John Brock, Park West's VP in charge of their VIP program. Up until that second, I had completely forgotten about that call and the ones that had followed, but I wasn't surprised. In addition to causing sleeplessness, heart palpitations, and mood swings, highly stressful situations or long periods of intense anxiety could also make people forget things.

A few weeks after the now-infamous cruise, Kelly and I received a phone call from John Brock. He had reached out to us after we left a bad review about the way certain Park West staff members treated us when we told them we couldn't buy every piece we'd won in the auctions.

During that call, Brock asked about the review and requested more details. I told him about their finance person, Lisa, and how rude she treated my wife and me. He was already well-versed in this situation, and he knew we'd been long-time VIP members and had invested quite a lot of money through Park West. I told him how shocked I'd been when a Park West employee had treated us so poorly. I also used the call as an opportunity to mention how inappropriate it was for members of his team to drink the way they had aboard the ship when their focus should have been on their business responsibilities. Maybe my tone of voice caught his attention because he asked me to tell him who I was talking about.

"First and foremost," I said, "Jordan and Katherine and a few other auctioneers, as well as Romero Britto."

WHY ME?

As soon as I mentioned Britto, I could sense his change of demeanor even through the phone.

He said, "Stop, I believe I can tell you what happened, but I'm going to let you tell me."

I didn't understand fully what he meant, but what I did get from his statement surprised me. I couldn't be completely sure, but he seemed to be indicating he had knowledge regarding Britto and his improper behavior.

It's upsetting to think they'd known what he was capable of and had still set him loose on their unsuspecting guests which made me ill, and I didn't want to discuss it anymore just then.

"When I'm ready to talk about my situation, I'll call you back." I disconnected the call without waiting for a response, then headed into the house to find my wife.

I told Kelly about the call and what Brock had said, and she agreed with what my instincts were telling me. In order for Brock to make a statement like that, he must have received calls and complaints about Britto, either before, during, or after our last cruise.

"You need to tell Mr. Brock what happened to you, Shawn," Kelly said.

I agreed. They needed to know.

About a week later, I called Brock and told him everything Romero Britto did and said in his cabin room that night. I cried as I described everything I'd had to endure, and Brock apologized his way through my entire story. When I finished, he offered to take back all the Britto paintings we had purchased over the years and give us a full refund for the price we had paid for them. He offered to pay for the shipping, as well.

"Thank you for listening," I said. "As for the paintings, I'll need to talk to my wife about your offer and get back to you."

"Also, if it was up to me we won't leave Britto alone again if he joins us on any future cruises, and we intend to stay by his side throughout the remainder of his showings with the gallery."

He sounded sincere and apologetic, and I thanked him once more and tried not to start crying again.

"Oh, and Shawn? One more thing... Whatever you decide to do about, well, you know...what happened with Britto? I'll support whatever decision you make."

"Thank you. Good-bye." I ended the call abruptly, no longer able to hold back my tears or the torrent of mixed emotions that caused my throat to constrict.

As I said, Brock's words of sympathy and his offer to buy back the paintings had sounded sincere. Now, I'm not so sure... A few weeks after that second call, I attempted to get in touch with him again, but I wasn't able to reach him. I called several times, and John Brock never picked up the phone again.

***

As our second day of protesting went on, more and more people approached us with stories about Romero Britto and his terrible character. One woman asked if she could stand with us in protest. She made fun of his talent—or, in her opinion, his lack of talent, and she said she thought his simple, cartoonish, amateur work received too much praise and people paid too much money for them. Obviously, she wasn't a fan.

Although the value of a piece of art is largely subjective and often depends on what someone is willing to pay to acquire it, her comments surprised me. After all, prior to the cruise, I had a great deal of admiration for his work, and I admired his talent. But as the day progressed, I discovered many other locals had similar opinions to the woman who'd thought Britto had no talent. Several people told us they felt like his artwork was meant more for tourists and not for the people who shared the beautiful city with him or lived in the Hispanic community. This brought to mind a video I had watched a few weeks before our protest. In the short clip, which ended up going viral, a Florida restaurateur was yelling at Romero Britto and smashing one of his paintings that she had purchased at a meet-and-greet event. The restaurant owner broke the expensive piece of art because allegedly, Britto had been disrespectful to her staff. The business owner went on to tell him, "Never go to my restaurant again and offend my people. I respect you as an artist." After the video went viral, a reporter tracked down the woman and did an interview. "I believe Romero Britto has forgotten where he came from and has lost touch with the Hispanic community because he is consumed by greed," she'd told the reporter.

As we protested, we heard the same or similar statements from many other people. In addition, I would add that not only had Britto lost sight of his community, he had lost sight of his humanity, as well. Hearing personal tales from people all over the Miami area only confirmed what I had learned way back in December.

Chapter 10

WE PROTESTED FOR two days outside Romero Britto's Art Gallery in Miami, Florida, and overall, we were met with a significant amount of support. As the second night ended, I began to feel some closure; a dim light shined at the end of the tunnel.

We gathered our t-shirts and picket signs and called it a day. I wanted to leave the city that had received us so warmly on a high note, so I treated my family and friends to dinner, and then we strolled alongside an outdoor market. We shopped for small trinkets and went out to a couple of proper art galleries. A warmth filled the air that evening, brought on by more than just the Florida heat. I felt mostly whole for the first time in a long time, and for the first time in the last seventy-two hours, I allowed myself to miss my mom. I felt as if her spirit guided me through my protest, and I wished she had been there with me. My mother and I were never close when I was growing up, but the three years we spent together later in life were beautiful, and I'd like to dedicate this book to her and to my upbringing. I grew up without a father figure and looked to people such as my teachers, coaches, principals, and pastors for guidance. I wouldn't be half the man I am today if it weren't for the strong sense of community that had been instilled in me and those friends, neighbors, and mentors who took the time to contribute to my life. I wouldn't have half the strength I have now if it weren't for what I've endured. I would have never found the strength to tell my story if it weren't for my endurance.

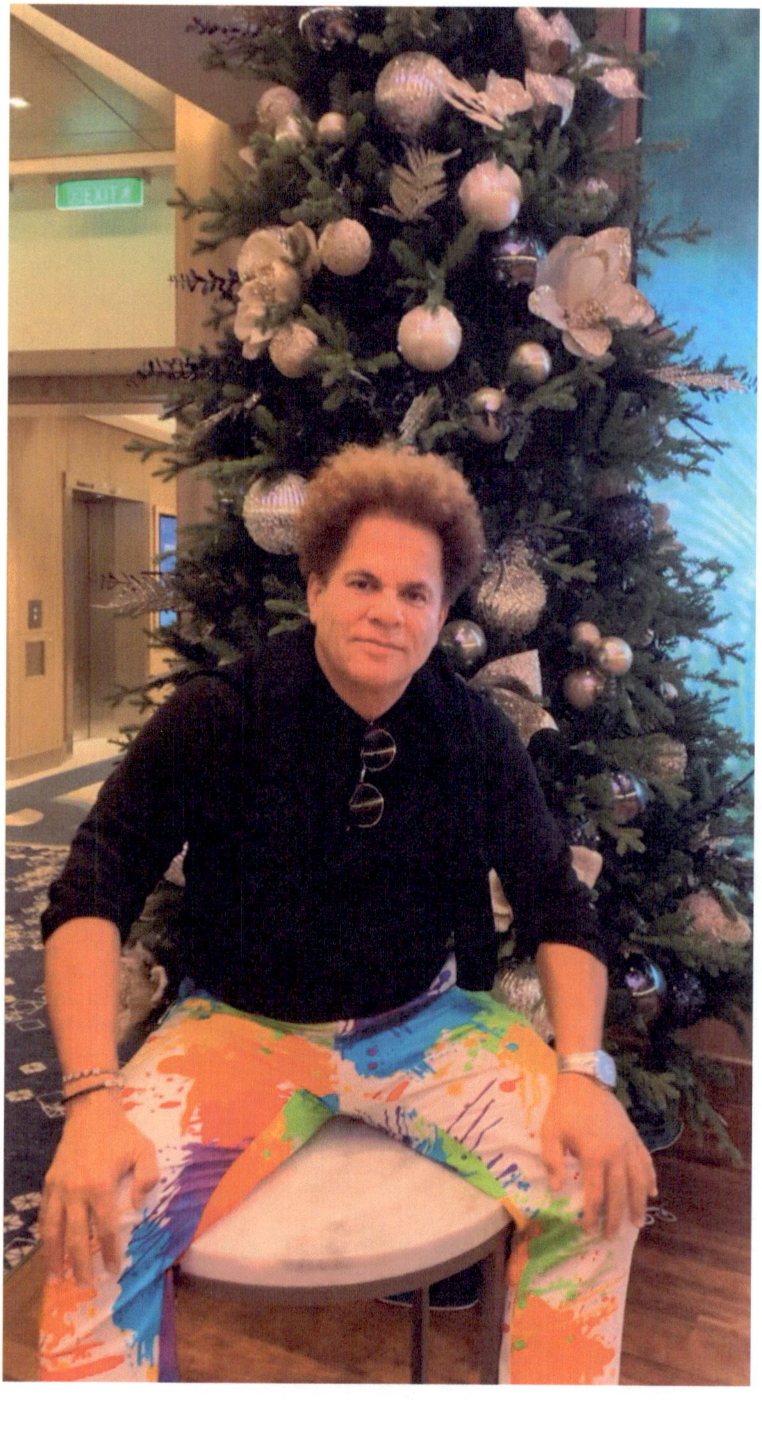
EXIT

Quotes

HERBERT "SHAWN" MILLER

"No Means No"

By saying nothing, it feels as if I am saying that

it is okay.

As a Black Man, I am speaking out today, It is

not okay.

No Means No.

WHY ME?

(FRONT)

No means No

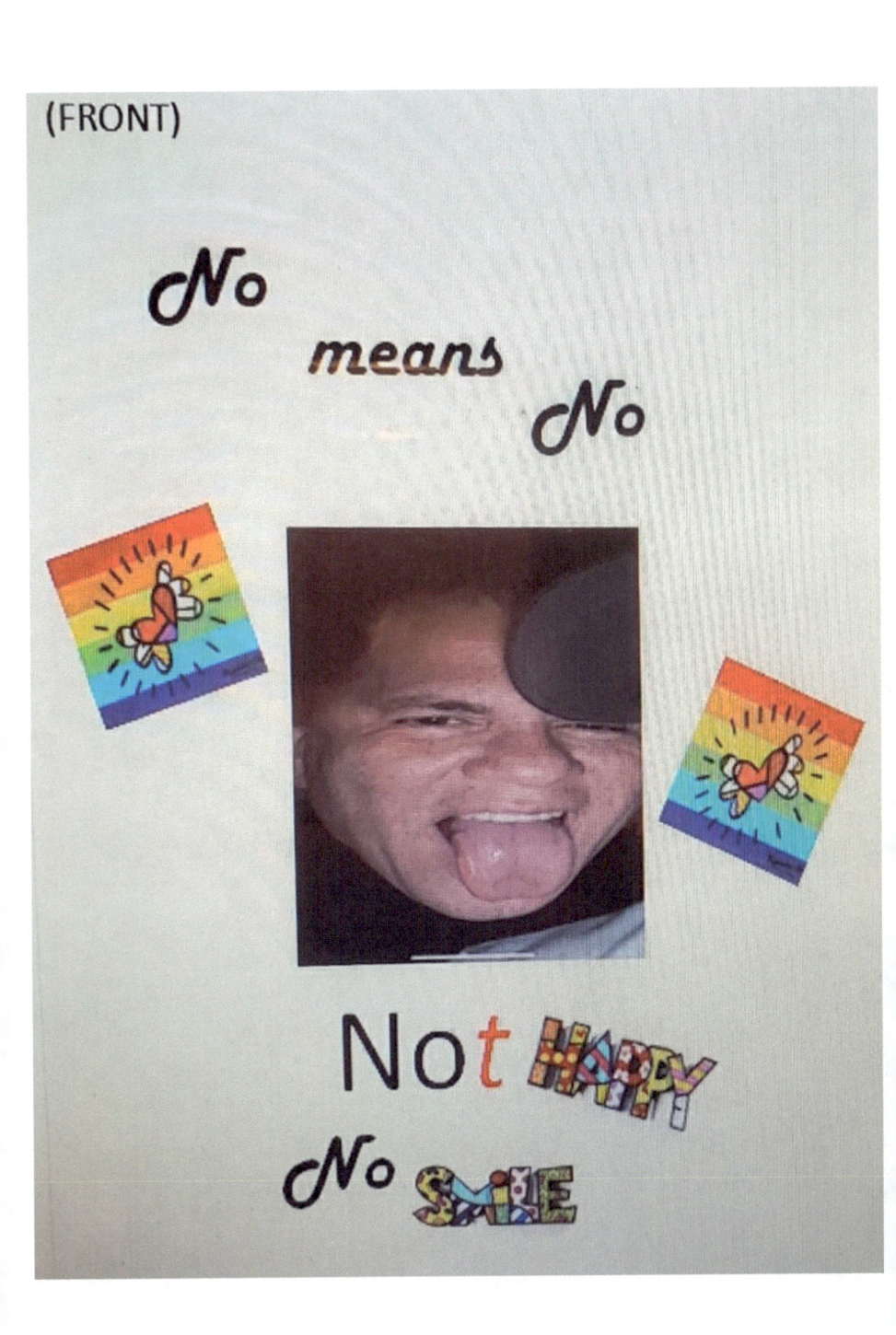

Not HAPPY
No SMILE

"There is no greater agony than the untold story

inside of you."

- Maya Angelou

Hold On

Do not let anyone suppress you; that is the only way you won't collapse.

Do not let anyone intimidate you, even if they are stronger than you.

Only then can you hold out and succeed.

Healing

An unhealed person can find offense in pretty much anything someone else does. But a healed person will understand that the actions of others have absolutely nothing to do with them. Each day we get to decide which one we will be.

Stronger

Because of my perpetrator, I am stronger

because I've had to be.

And I am wiser from my mistakes.

I am happier due to my sadness.

And with this knowledge, I am a survivor.

Winning

To be a winner, you have to stand out from the crowd. This will require one to stand up for what they believe in, So don't let fear silence you. You are a winner.

You Can't Hide

Barbarity: used behind their status, their fame, their notoriety, and their hypocrisy.

Floating

After an assault, you can't feel. I'm not here.

I'm in the air. In the ocean. I'm everywhere.

Nowhere.